GREEK
ISLANDS

PAUL HARCOURT DAVIES

NEW
HOLLAND

NEW
HOLLAND

★★★ Highly recommended
★★ Recommended
★ See if you can

This edition first published in 2001
by New Holland Publishers (UK) Ltd
London • Cape Town • Sydney • Auckland
First published in 1997
10 9 8 7 6 5

website: www.newhollandpublishers.com

Garfield House, 86 Edgware Road
London W2 2EA, United Kingdom

80 McKenzie Street, Cape Town 8001
South Africa

14 Aquatic Drive, Frenchs Forest, NSW 2086
Australia

218 Lake Road, Northcote, Auckland
New Zealand

Distributed in the USA by
The Globe Pequot Press
Connecticut

ISBN 1 85974 754 X

Committioning Editor: Tim Jollands
Manager Globetrotter Maps: John Loubser
Production: Myrna Collins
Managing Editor: Thea Grobbelaar
Editor: Nune Jordaan, Tarryn Berry
Picture Researcher: Emily Hedges, Sonya Meyer
Design and DTP: Sonya Cupido
Cartographer: Éloïse Moss
Compiler/Verifier: Genené Dickson
Reproduction by Hirt & Carter (Pty) Ltd, Cape Town
Printed and bound in Hong Kong by Sing Cheong
Printing Co. Ltd.

Photographic Credits:
David Alexander, page 120 (bottom); John Frick,
pages 18, 65, 108; Paul Harcourt Davies, pages 8, 9,
10, 11; Life File/Dr R. Cannon, page 61; Life File/
Jeremy Hoare, pages 36, 53; Life File/Barry Mayes,
page 63; Andreas Nicola, pages 27, 28; PhotoBank/
Jeanetta Baker, page 44; PhotoBank/Peter Baker,
pages 21, 45, 72, 77, 82, 104, 105, 114, 120 (top);
PhotoBank/Gary Goodwin, pages 17, 33 (bottom), 34,
86; Picture Bank Photo Library (PBPL), pages 7, 14,
24, 52 (top), 89, 91, 97; Robert Harding Picture
LIbrary (RHPL), title page, pages 4, 20, 40, 42, 43, 62,
75, 93, 103 (top and bottom), 107, 110, 118, 119; RHPL/
David Beatty, pages 26, 100; RHPL/F. Dubes, page 94;
RHPL/Robert Francis, page 60; RHPL/Lee Frost,
page 48; RHPL/Tony Gervis, page 30; RHPL/Michael
Jenner, pages 15, 96; RHPL/G. Kavallierakis,
pages 50, 56, 68, 117; RHPL/J. Lightfoot, page 59;
RHPL/Roy Rainford, page 33 (top); RHPL/Rolf
Richardson, page 106; RHPL/Michael Short, page 78
(top); RHPL/E. Simanor, page 92; RHPL/Susan
Griggs Agency, page 58; RHPL/G. White, page 19;
RHPL/Rob Whitrow, pages 64, 76, 78 (bottom), 90;
RHPL/Adam Woolfitt, page 12; Peter Ryan, pages 16,
25, 29; Spectrum Colour Library, page 109; Travel
Ink/Ian Booth, pages 81, 83; Travel Ink/Nigel Bowen-
Morris, pages 6, 35; Travel Ink/Ann Curtis, page 52
(bottom); Travel Ink/Guy Marks, pages 22, 23; Peter
Wilson, cover; ZEFA, page 111.

Although every effort has been made to ensure
accuracy of facts, telephone and fax numbers in this
book, the publishers will not be held responsible for
changes that occur at the time of going to press.

Cover: View of Mýkanos harbour, Cyclades.
Title Page: Yachts line the quay in Sými harbour.

Note:
In the transliteration of place names from Greek to
English spellings, various authors have tried to
convey Greek sounds in different ways. The Greek
gamma is not a simple 'g' but is more gutteral or can
have a 'y' sound. thus many different spellings are
encountered. For example, Ayios meaning 'saint', and
used in all church names (e.g. Ayios Yióryiou) can also
be spelt Aghios or Agios. Similarly 'dh' is sometimes
used to convey the soft 'th' sound of a Greek delta –
elsewhere you might find a simple 'd'.

CONTENTS

1
Introducing the Greek Islands

Escape...to a gentle pace of life in a world of tiny villages where whitewashed houses cascade down hillsides towards azure-blue seas and the sun always shines – that is the popular message of the Greek Islands in fable and films from *Zorba the Greek* to *Shirley Valentine*.

The Greek islands are, by convention, divided into distinct groups – **Saronic Islands**, **Cyclades**, **Ionian Isles**, **Dodecanese**, **Northeastern Aegean** and the **Sporades**. Island hopping, using the extensive network of ferries, is easy and a real delight – the variety of character and lifestyle offered by the islands extends from the bustling popularity of **Rhodes** and **Corfu**, which cater for the masses, to isolated islands such as **Síkinos** where escape becomes a reality.

The culture of Greece has left indelible marks on the whole of Western Civilization through its literature, art, architecture, philosophy and the first experiments with democracy. The sea has always been part of this culture, and nowhere more so than on the islands which have long acted as stepping stones between Asia and Europe.

Most visitors travel to the islands during **July** and **August** when the weather can be very hot. Naturalists and walkers will prefer **April** and **May** when the flowers are in bloom, while **October** is a great time for those who want warmth, peace and quiet. Although the larger islands can be reached by direct flights and ferries all year round, regular services to smaller, isolated islands do not begin until the summer crowds arrive, and tend to finish at the end of **September**.

TOP ATTRACTIONS

*** Athens: Acropolis and Parthenon – the most famous temple in Greece.
*** Corfu: the magnificent Venetian town.
** Délos: the lions and other antiquities of the centre of worship in ancient Greece.
** Rhodes: Street of the Knights and the wonderful Medieval architecture.
** Skiáthos: renowned for the best beaches in Greece.
** Thíra (Santoríni): Akrotíri and the Minoan town.
* Crete: Knossós – painted remains of a Minoan city.

Opposite: *Island churches are distinctive with domes and whitewashed walls.*

FACT FILE

The islands make up some 25,000km² (10,000 sq miles) of the Greek landmass. There are over 1400 islands (perhaps 3000 if you count the isolated 'rocks') under Greek rule of which 160 or so are inhabited.
   Regular scheduled ferries connect 78 islands with a further 40 accessible via local boats which mainly operate in the summer months. Those islands that remain are inhabited by goat herds, monks and occasionally by the families of super-rich shipping magnates.

Below: *White houses perched on dizzy cliffs make an indelible impression on visitors arriving by boat (Oía town, Thíra).*

THE LAND

Although the Greek islands tend to be grouped for administrative and tourist convenience, each island retains a strong identity, particularly as far as proud islanders are concerned. Islands in the west (**Ionian**) and northeast (**Aegean**) lie near huge land masses, receive more winter rain and appear lush and green in comparison with the dry **Cyclades** and their wild, bare landscapes of limestone and sandstone rocks. A few islands – **Thíra** (Santoríni) is the best known – possess a lunar landscape of dark volcanic rocks. The higher mountains – more than 1500m (4922ft) – are confined to the larger islands (**Crete, Kefaloniá**,) but most of the islands are hilly, some of the smaller ones being little more than the tops of mountains, left when the **Mediterranean** basin was flooded in the distant past.

Many islands remained forested until around 8000 years ago – the dawn of 'civilization': today each island is a mosaic of habitats shaped by human intervention. Yet, the scrub-covered hillsides and poor soils which feature so much in the Greek-speaking world, are botanical treasure houses from which over 6000 species of flowering plants have been recorded.

Seas and Shores

Greek beaches are officially public although some beach hotels act as if their strip is not. On some islands beaches are designated for nude bathing – in practice, away from towns many visitors bare all.

Superb, sandy beaches are found on **Rhodes, Náxos, Skiáthos** and many other islands. There are tiny coves, seemingly endless stretches of golden sands, some crowded, others barely discovered – something for everyone.

Greece boasts over 14,500km (9000 miles) of coastline but there is little shallow water around the islands, except close to the shoreline. The **Ionian Sea**, the central basin of the **Mediterranean**, is well over 3500m (11,484ft) deep in a few places. By comparison, the **Aegean** is a shallower sea where winds create hazardous conditions which can make landing on rocky coasts a nightmare. Sensibly, the sailors of ancient Greece largely abandoned voyages during the winter months. The strong winds are encountered between April and October and during peak holiday times, providing some relief from high temperatures rather than proving a nuisance.

Above: *Mountains provide a backdrop to many Greek villages – nowhere more dramatically than Crete where the White Mountains are snow-capped for much of the year.*

Climate

The **Mediterranean** climate is characterized by mild, damp winters and hot, dry summers separated by short spring and autumn periods. Most **rain** falls in the winter and early spring months (**December to mid-March**). **Snow** occurs regularly only on the higher mountains. The climate of individual islands show variations: the northeastern Aegean islands have a slightly cooler, wetter climate than islands in the south while the islands to the west are noticeably drier than those in the eastern part.

COMPARATIVE CLIMATE CHART	IONIAN ISLES				AEGEAN ISLES				CYCLADES			
	SUM JAN	AUT APR	WIN JULY	SPR OCT	SUM JAN	AUT APR	WIN JULY	SPR OCT	SUM JAN	AUT APR	WIN JULY	SPR OCT
AVERAGE TEMP. °C	10	15	27	19	10	16	27	19	12	17	25	20
AVERAGE TEMP. °F	50	59	81	66	50	61	81	66	54	63	77	68
SEA TEMP. °C	13	16	24	22	11	14	25	21	15	16	24	21
SEA TEMP. °F	55	60	75	71	52	57	77	70	59	61	75	70
HOURS SUN	4	7	12	7	4	7	12	7	5	7	12	7
RAINFALL in	4.5	2.5	0	4	3	2	1	3	2.5	1	0	1.5
RAINFALL mm	111	62	6	105	71	48	19	73	66	18	1	36

A SALTY TALE

The **Mediterranean** sea loses far more water by evaporation than it gains from all the rivers which drain into it: the difference is replaced by a steady inflow of nutrient-rich sea water from the **Atlantic**. Thus, when visitors say it is easier to swim in the Mediterranean they are right: evaporation increases the salt content and this creates a greater degree of buoyancy.

High temperatures in **July** and **August** are made tolerable throughout the islands by the *meltémi*. This wind begins as a breeze at dawn, rises to a crescendo around midday and falls almost imperceptibly towards evening. Sailors in north-facing bays need to set sail early or face being trapped until the wind dies down.

Winds have long dictated the ease of passage between the islands and the most effective sea routes. Hot summer air brings the *Etesian* winds which once filled the sails of Mycenaean ships: boats were hauled ashore in autumn and then re-launched in spring when the lesser *Prodroms* began to blow. The *Etesian* winds give a clarity and brisk-ness to the Aegean air and wonderfully clear night skies. Ionian skies have a hint of haze about them in summer. In spring and autumn the *Sirocco* blows: in its travels it collects moisture increasing humidity (and human lethargy). The *Gregale* is a winter wind of moist Atlantic air that brings heavy squalls in the Ionian islands, rapidly darkening clear skies and forcing fishermen close to shore.

Plant Life

The study of Greek plant life began with the philosopher Aristotle in the 4th century BC. One of his brilliant pupils, Theophrastus, wrote on orchids and is regarded as the first true botanist, while Dioscorides wrote his well-known *Materia Medica* on the medicinal uses of plants in the first century AD.

Below: *Spring brings a rush of colour to the fields such as those near Aradhena in Crete.*
Opposite: *Bright pink Judas trees in blossom.*

Many of the plants of mainland Greece are also found on the islands. In addition, isolation has given some plants the time to evolve and become quite distinct from their mainland relatives. Extensive **saltmarsh** and **sand dune** areas are unusual in the islands, yet sandy soils within a few metres of the sea shore have **yellow horned poppies**, **purple sea stock**, **scarlet poppies** and, in the height of summer, **white sea lilies**. Large cultivated areas are as sterile in Greece as they are elsewhere whereas small, stony fields are a haven of species, forming an astonishingly colourful patchwork of **white chamomile**, **yellow crown daisies**, **scarlet poppies** and splashes of **blue anchusa**.

Phrygana (*garigue*) – low, scented scrub – colours the hills in spring when the woody herbs (oregano, thyme and sage) and **rockroses** (*cistus*) flower. Hillsides are dotted with the thin, dark forms of the **funeral cypress** and enlivened by springtime splashes of pink when the **Judas trees** flower. Phrygana is succeeded by taller bushes and small trees of the **maquis** (mastic, strawberry tree, myrtle) and then by open woodlands of **Aleppo pine** (*Pinus bratia*) with an under-storey of shrubs. Significant forest areas still occur on some of the larger islands (Chíos, Sámos, Lésbos). Mt Aínos on Kefaloniá (1620m; 5315ft) is thickly wooded with **Greek silver fir** (*Abies cephalonica*). Elsewhere, **Aleppo pine** is the dominant species on lower mountains, giving way to the **black pine** (*Pinus nigra*).

Only Crete has mountains high enough to possess a genuine high-mountain component in its flora: **Cretan crocus** (*Crocus sieberi*), **Cretan chionodoxia** (*Chionodoxa cretica*), mats of a striking, blue **bugloss** (*Anchusa caespitosa*) and the **Ida arum** (*Arum idaeum*) among many others.

Conserving the Natural Heritage

Greece has in recent years become active in conservation even though some of its famous sons were writing about the denudation of hills and dangers of erosion over 2000 years ago. The small but dedicated membership of the **Hellenic Society for the Protection of Nature** (9 Kidathineon Street, Athens) has been a driving force.

BULBS

Stony fields and scrubby hillsides on lime-rich soils offer an array of bulbous plants which appear with the first rains. The autumn-flowering species: yellow **sternbergias** and pink **colchicums** bring welcome colour to parched hillsides, yet the main explosion occurs in spring time.

In the far southern islands spring begins as early as February with the first rush of **anemones** followed by **grape hyacinths** (*muscari*), **crocuses**, **irisis**, **tulips** and then vast numbers of annual species – the Aegean islands have a distinctly 'eastern' flavour to their bulb flora.

WILD ORCHIDS

Some species of wild orchids, especially the genus *ophrys*, mimic insects in shape, colour and scent in order to attract them for pollination. These orchids draw numerous enthusiasts to the islands each year – favourite destinations are Crete, Corfu, Rhodes, Lésbos and Sámos. Crete alone boasts nearly 70 species of wild orchid including the **Cretan bee orchid** (*Ophrys cretica*) and the **hooded helleborine** (*Cephalanthera cucullata*) that are found nowhere else in the world. On Lésbos a few plants of the rare and beautiful **Komper's orchid** (*Comperia comperiana*) grow in the mountains.

Because of the mountainous nature of much of its territory Greece has largely escaped the ravages of intensive cultivation with the attendant cocktail of pesticides and herbicides. Around the cities and major ports pollution is at danger levels and on some islands over-development for tourism has destroyed many rich habitats. There are 10 areas in Greece designated as national parks (three on the islands) but little in the way of a sub-structure of wardens and rangers to care for them (Crete's Samariá Gorge is the exception). On a positive note, environmentalists are pushing for legislation and the seas around the northern Sporades have been designated a national marine park. Efforts are also being made to protect the endangered **monk seal**, **green** and **loggerhead turtles** and **Eleanora's falcon**.

Wildlife

In the Pleistocene period, some of the bigger islands were home to the **dwarf elephant**, **pygmy hippopotamus**, **ibex**, **genet** and **wild boar**. Today, hunting and de-forestation have almost driven the last of the larger mammals from the islands, although **badger**, **fox**, **beech marten**, **weasel** and **hare** have survived in isolated areas. The **kri-kri**, or Cretan ibex, has a stronghold in the White Mountains of Crete and on its offshore islands (Dhía and Agios Theódori). Crete also has an endemic animal – the **Cretan spiny mouse** (*Acomys minous*), which is unique to Crete and has spines rather than hairs on its back. It is an inhabitant of rocky hillsides. The most widespread Mediterranean cetacean is the **common dolphin**, often seen in schools 'surfing' the bow waves of ferries. **Bottle-nosed dolphins** are also often spotted.

For the birdwatcher the best times to visit coincide with the spring (April–mid-May) and autumn (late August–September) migrations, though these are

Below: *Tree frogs, although rather small, make a noise out of all proportion to their size.*

never easy to predict. In spring there are vividly coloured **hoopoes**, **rollers** and **bee-eaters** as well as a host of small **warblers**. At lake margins large water birds include **herons**, **bitterns** and **egrets**. In the White Mountains of Crete look out for the four European species of vulture including the **lammergeier** (bearded vulture) and **blue rock thrush**. **Eleanora's falcons** raise their broods to catch the autumn migration on islands off the north coast and come to Sitía to feed.

From April onwards **butterflies** appear: **swallowtails** both common and scarce, **southern festoons** (Crete has an endemic festoon) and a yellow, brimstone relative with bright orange patches – the **Cleopatra**. **Hawkmoths** are common – especially the tiny whirring forms of the **hummingbird hawk** which flies by day. **Jersey tiger moths** are found on most of the islands but in Rhodes they were responsible for the famous displays at Petaloúdhes (Butterfly Valley, *see* p. 92).

You may spot a **praying mantis** or **adult cicada** on a tree branch although they are more easily heard than seen. Malaria has been eradicated but **mosquitoes** are still a pest – try locally sold repellents, liquids and plug-in machines to prevent irritating bites.

The **blunt-nose viper** (*Vipera lebetina*) is the only snake dangerous to humans; it has a distinctive yellow, horn-like tail. Lizards are seemingly everywhere, from tiny pale geckos to the large **Balkan green lizards** (*Lacerta trilineata*). Tiny, green **tree frogs** (*Hyla arborea*), can be heard at night in the trees: in spring any pond is alive with vocal **marsh frogs** (*Rana ridibunda*), and you might hear the 'plop' of a submerging **striped-necked terrapin** (*Mauremys caspica*) as you approach.

Island beaches tend not to be rich in shells but close to shore **sea urchins**, colourful **peacock wrasses** and scarlet **soldier fish** can be seen when snorkelling.

Above: *The swallowtail, one of the most colourful of all Greek butterflies.*

TURTLES

Two decades ago some 1500 loggerhead turtles (*Caretta caretta*) nested annually on the sandy beaches of Zákinthos: now their numbers have been more than halved as tourist pressure has driven them from Laganás Bay to other beaches. Power boats and jet skis can cut them, plastic bags choke them and, at night, beach lights or activity prevent them from emerging to lay their eggs. Hatchlings are extremely vulnerable as they crawl to the sea. Luckily a dedicated group of people is fighting to make sure turtles and tourists co-exist.

If you are interested in helping, write to the **Sea Turtle Protection Society of Greece**, PO Box 511, 54 Kifissia, 14510 Greece.

Above: *Délos, a religious and commercial centre in Classical times.*

HISTORY IN BRIEF

Evidence of human activity in Greece stretches as far back as 8500BC to proto-Greek settlers from the eastern **Mediterranean**. The peoples of **Crete** and the **Cyclades** were constructing superb palaces around 3000BC.

Early Cycladic 4500–2000BC

The islands were colonized and small agrarian and fishing communities were established. The first traces of a 'civilization' have been found in the **Cyclades**, where a distinct culture flourished from 3200–2000BC until trading brought in outside influences. Its main legacy is the small marble figurines found in tombs.

Minoan 2000–1500BC

The Bronze age Minoans were the first major power in the Aegean – with great palaces on **Crete** at Knossós, Phaistós, Zákros, Mália, Chaniá and the ancient settlement of Akrotíri on **Thíra**. Agriculture underpinned the **Minoan** economy and enabled them to indulge a passion for art. Minoan civilization literally came tumbling down in 1500BC when Thíra, the nearest of the Cyclades, exploded in a volcanic eruption.

Mycenaean and the Dark Ages 1500–776BC

The Mycenaeans from the Peloponnese also evolved a successful palace-ruled civilization: they succeeded the Minoans and absorbed a great deal of that culture. Essentially a military people, their weapons and funeral artefacts were nevertheless richly decorated with gold and jewels. They built a trading empire across the eastern **Mediterranean** and became embroiled in a 10-year war against Troy. **Dorians**, often regarded as 'barbarians', invaded from the north in 1100BC: palaces fell and trading was interrupted. **Phoenician** traders revitalized those islands which lay on their trade routes: Greek culture began to flourish, city states arose and the Olympic Games were established in 776BC.

Archaic Period 776–490BC

This was a dynamic and experimental period before art became 'Classical'. Greek architecture borrowed ideas of scale and the use of supporting columns from Egyptian builders but evolved the elegant lines associated with later Classical buildings: statues and carvings, too, began to take on realistic rather than representational proportions. A number of islands came into prominence as powerful island states. **Àegína's** silver coins became a common currency in much of the Mediterranean. **Délos** achieved renown as the shrine to Apollo. **Sámos** became a democracy in 650BC, then the tyrant Polykrates assumed power in 550BC and became the first to rule the Aegean since King Minos. The people of **Sífnos** were reputed to be the wealthiest in Greece because of the gold and silver mined there. **Thíra** began to mint its own coinage in the 6th century and its influence extended not only to Crete, Rhodes and Páros but also to Mílos. Persian attacks on the

---

CULTURE VULTURES

The cultural explosion associated with Classical Greek civilization was centred on Athens: **Aristophanes** wrote his comedies, **Aeschylus**, **Euripedes** and **Sophocles** penned great dramatic plays, **Phidias** created sculptures, **Socrates** founded a whole school of philosophical thought later developed by **Plato**. The islands produced their important figures, too. **Hippocrates** (Kos – father of medicine), **Pythagoras** (Sámos – mathematician and philosopher) and **Sappho** (Lésbos – poetess).

HISTORICAL CALENDAR

7000–2800BC Neolithic Era.
4000 Settlements on Límnos.
3000–2000 Early Cycladic.
2800–1000 Bronze Age.
2600–2000 Early Minoan culture in Crete.
2000–1700 Middle Minoan – Crete major sea power.
1700–1450 Late Minoan Age.
1600–1150 Mycenaeans rule in Peloponnese: occupy Crete and Rhodes.
1150 Dorian invasion: Ionian settlement of Aegean Islands and Asia Minor. Start of the Dark Age in Greece.
500–323 Classical Age, Parthenon finished.
478 Délos made the centre of a Maritime league.
431–404 Athens crippled by Peloponnese war.
378 Second Délian League .
338 Greece conquered by Philip of Macedon.

334–323 Alexander the Great establishes his empire.
180BC–AD395 Roman Age.
AD395 Byzantine Period.
AD58 St Paul visits Lindos.
95 St John writes Revelations on Patmos.
824–861 Saracen/Arab occupation of the islands.
1204 Fall of Constantinople – Venetians control islands.
1261 Constantinople taken by Greeks from Latins.
1309 Rhodes becomes base for Knights of St John.
1453 Turkish conquest of Greece begins.
1522 Knights of St John defeated by Ottomans.
1669 Venetians lose Iráklion (Crete) to Turks.
1796 Napoleon captures Venice and Ionian Islands.
1815–64 Ionian Islands under British Rule.

1821–27 Greek War of Independence.
1912–13 Greece gains Crete and northeast Aegean Islands in Balkan Wars – Dodecanese islands gained by Italy.
1922–23 Greece invades Turkey. Brutal reprisals.
1941 Germany invades Crete.
1948 Dodecanese returned.
1949 Civil war ends.
1953 Earthquake devastates Ionian islands.
1967 CIA-backed Colonels *coup d'état* establishes Junta.
1974 Junta falls. Turkey invades Cyprus.
1981 PASOK 'Socialist' government elected.
1990 PASOK lose elections to Néa Dhimokratía. Mitsotakis becomes prime minister.
1993 PASOK re-elected.
1996 Kostas Simitis replaces Papandreou as prime minister.

THE CYPRUS QUESTION

The Turks with Britain and
Greece were appointed
'guarantor powers' after
Cyprus gained independence
from Britain in 1964. The
Turks had long threatened
to invade Cyprus to 'protect'
the Turkish minority and the
action by the Colonels (see p.
17) provided an ideal excuse.
  Greeks were forced from
the north – the invasion
was brutal and condemned
internationally. Since 1974
the island has remained
partitioned with the north
recognized as a state only
by Turkey. Since the invasion
many Turkish Cypriots have
left the north and its economy
is faltering, while that of the
south has flourished.

islands became reality until they were repelled by the
Athenian-led army at **Marathon** (490BC) and in the naval
battle of Salamis (480BC). Athens became a powerful
maritime force, and because the Aegean islands had been
considerably weakened by Persian attacks, they struck a
deal with Athens offering to pay money in return for protection. Known as the **Delian League**, the allowance was
exploited by Athens which took marble from the islands,
while Pericles used the protection money of the Delian
League to pay for the construction of the Parthenon.

  Other city states (**Corinth** and **Sparta**) challenged
the supremacy of Athens during the Peloponnese War
(431– 404BC) but the major players all emerged too
weakened to claim any dominance.

Classical and Hellenistic 490–180BC
Alexander the Great accomplished Greek unification
in 336BC, marking the transition from the Classical to
Hellenistic period. Alexander's empire extended to India
and Egypt but on his death from fever at the early age of
33, it was fragmented by rivalries among his generals. Art

flourished along lines established in the
Classical period, becoming more ornate.
Sámos and **Rhodes** established reputations
as centres of learning to rival Athens.

Roman Period 180BC–AD395
Rome first gained a foothold in the islands
as an arbiter in disputes. By 31BC the
Roman Empire encompassed the whole
of Greece, with the islands divided among
five provinces: Epirus embraced the
Ionian Islands; Asia, the eastern Aegean
islands and the Dodecanese; Cyrenica-
Creta included Crete with Libya, while
Thásos went with Macedonia and Achaea
included Evia along with the Peloponnese.

  The Romans laid roads, built aqueducts
and refurbished towns. Wealthy Romans
took to visiting the islands, even

schooling their sons there and carrying away beautiful statues and carvings to adorn their homes. **Pausanias**, a Roman, wrote the first 'travel guide' to Greece in AD150.

Byzantine Period
AD395–AD1453
The islands faced a millennium of attacks from invaders. Their proximity to the Greek coast made the **Ionian** islands important staging posts: **Corfu** was attacked by Goths and Vandals in the 5th century and then conquered by Normans in the 12th century. After Constantinople (present day Istanbul) fell, the islands were given to noble Venetian families as fiefdoms: **Venetian** rule held in the face of **Ottoman** attacks until the islands were gained by **France** under Napoleon Bonaparte in 1797.

Major trade routes to Smyrna (present day Turkish Izmir) and Aleppo (in Syria) lay via Crete and the eastern Aegean islands: the Cyclades were largely neglected and were abandoned or became the lair of pirates. Venetian rule of a kind came after 1204 when **Marco Sanudo** founded the Duchy of the Archipelago on **Náxos**.

Arab pirates originally targeted the **Aegean** islands as well as the **Cyclades**. **Crete's** strategic position made it a target for Saracen invaders. Venice regarded Crete as its most important outpost but after the Ottoman conquest many families nominally converted to Islam. The Colossus of Rhodes, toppled by an earthquake in 225BC, was removed for scrap by Saracen invaders in AD634. After the fourth Crusade the Genoese were granted sole rights to colonize the eastern **Aegean** and trade with Black Sea ports. From 1204 **Rhodes** first came under Frankish and then Venetian rule. The Knights of St John maintained

Above: *The medical centre – the Asklepeion on Kos was a place of pilgrimage in Classical times.*
Opposite: *Some of the glory of the Minoan period is revealed at Knossós. Controversial archaeologist, Sir Arthur Evans restored and painted the ruins as they might have been.*

SHIPPING

World shipping was once dominated by mega-rich Greek families (such as Onassis, Niarchos, Goulandris) and was an important source of revenue for the country. It was devastated by a world recession in the 1980s and at the same time tourism fell dramatically after Americans refused to travel via Athens airport – considered an easy target for terrorists.

Above: *Greek churches such as that at Andri, Crete, are a treasure house of Christian art.*

their headquarters on Rhodes until the Ottoman siege. Curiously, both **Sými** and **Kálimnos** prospered under the Ottomans through their sponge fishing.

Ottoman Rule 1453–1832

Islands closest to the Turkish coast fell first to the Ottomans but the period of acquisition was a lengthy one – from 1522 **(Rhodes)** to 1715 **(Tínos)**.

Russia held control over a dozen or so islands during its war against Turkey from 1770–74 . As Turkish might declined there was an upsurge of Greek nationalism: such insurrection inevitably brought reprisals (in the worst of them 25,000 people were massacred in 1822 on Chíos).

Independence

Independence came in 1832 but with it Greece only gained control of the **Cyclades**. Britain transferred **Corfu** and the **Ionian** Islands to Greek rule (1860s) and the **Northern Aegean** Islands were regained at the end of World War I. The **Dodecanese** were in Italian hands from 1912 and taken over by Germany in 1943. In 1947 the Dodecanese passed from Allied to Greek control.

In 1909 the Cretan statesman, Eleftherios Venizelos, formed a new Liberal government. From 1912–13 he led an alliance which fought in the Balkan Wars until Greece entered **World War I** on the side of the Allies. In 1920 monarchist factions forced action against Mustafa Kemal or Atatürk in Ankara (Turkey) which proved disastrous for Greece. In 1923 almost 400,000 Muslims (mainly from the islands) left Greece and were 'exchanged' for about 1.3 million Greeks. Those Greeks and millions of Armenians left in Turkey were systematically and brutally exterminated.

General Ioánnis Metaxás, appointed prime minister of Greece in 1936 by King George II, established a state based on fascist lines, but completely opposed Italian or German domination. Greek forces drove Italian invaders from the country in 1940 but the next year German forces conquered the mainland and islands. By the end of 1941 German troops had occupied **Crete** and the islanders were brutally punished for their determined resistance. Nearly 500,000 Greeks starved to death when food was taken for the occupying armies and almost the entire population of Jews was deported to concentration camps.

From 1945–49 Greece became embroiled in a bloody civil war between communist and monarchist forces, with the latter, American-backed, emerging as the victors. On 21 April 1967, a CIA-backed *coup d'état* brought the 'Colonels' to power. Their repressive, fascist regime ended (1974) when they attempted to topple Makarios III in **Cyprus** as a diversionary tactic to recreate a tide of nationalist support. Their efforts failed when Makarios escaped and the Turks were given an excuse to invade **Cyprus** – which they did with unforgivable brutality – it has remained partitioned since. From 1974 Greece has, once again, enjoyed democratic rule; the monarchy was formally abolished in 1975.

> ### THE COLONELS
>
> The Junta's aim was a moral cleansing of Greece – human rights were ignored and censorship became ridiculous. Dissidents and their families were imprisoned and tortured by the secret police: many disappeared. On 17 November 1973, students at the Athens Polytechnic went on strike – the rebellion was quelled with tanks and many died. Papadopoulos, head of the secret police, was arrested. His successor, Ioannides, tried to unite the country on a wave of nationalism by assassinating Makarios and uniting Cyprus with Greece. It failed – the Junta fell and Karamanlis returned from exile in France to form a government.

Below: *Evzone guards on duty at the Tomb of the Unknown Soldier, Athens.*

WOMEN'S RIGHTS

A woman's right to vote was not granted universally until 1956. PASOK fought both its elections (1981 and 1985) with a strong programme for Women's Rights. Extensive changes in family law were achieved in 1983 when equal legal status and property rights were granted to both husband and wife and the dowry custom was prohibited. Women's cooperatives have also been set up to help empower women (see p. 19).

Below: *Fertile plains between scrub-covered mountains are intensively cultivated on the islands.*
Opposite: *Waterways bustle with activity.*

GOVERNMENT AND ECONOMY

Greece has enjoyed a period of relative political stability since 1974 with a French-style presidency and a parliament with 300 seats. The main contenders for the people's vote are the right-wing **Néa Dhimokratía** (New Democracy), **Pan Hellenic Socialist Movement** (PASOK) and the **Communists** (KKE). The majority is currently held by PASOK – its leader was, until January 1996, the prime minister, Andreas Papandreou. He had, in recent years, survived numerous potentially embarrassing 'U' turns on policy and election promises together with more than a hint of scandal over his personal life. Questions about the sale of corn to the EU, embezzlement of deposits from the bank of Crete and suspect arms deals to which his name was linked brought the defeat of PASOK in November 1989. **Konstantinos Mitsotakis** replaced **Papandreou** but only until 1993. Papandreou retired in 1996 due to illness and later died. His post has been filled by **Kostas Simitis**.

The arrival of **Albanian** and **Serbian** refugees has not helped the economy and has created an underclass of cheap, exploitable labour and a scapegoat for society's ills.

Industry and Agriculture

Greece, a member of the EU since 1981, has one of the weakest European economies and endemic **high inflation**. The fall of the *drachma* against other currencies has made it good value for visitors and **tourism** is now vital to the economy for the foreign exchange it brings and the numbers of people employed – particularly on islands.

Greece has argued with its EU partners over the territorial issue of Macedonia; American bases (opposed for political expediency but in reality a money-earner) are closing – except for Soudha Bay on Crete; and Greece is no longer a top tourist destination. Greece has set its sights on the 'quality' end of the market but without the necessary investment to effect the change.

On the islands, cen-
turies-old methods of
agriculture are being
abandoned, rather than
modernized, as young
people eschew the hard
life on the land and head
for cities. On the larger
islands, agriculture is the
mainstay of the economy –
olives and **citrus** fruit
form the major component
for home consumption and
for export. Locally, crops

like **tomatoes**, **peppers** (and on Aegína, **pistachio nuts**)
and **fishing** can generate vital income. Manufacturing
industry is essentially low-key (**clothing**, **shoes**, **electrical
goods**), mainland-based and largely for the home market.

There is definitely an omnipresent tension with Turkey
(an issue uniting all parties) not only over the latter's
intransigence concerning the 'Cyprus question' (*see* p. 14),
but also its refusal to recognize Greek rights to **oil** beneath
the Aegean seabed. The volatility of the relationship was
shown in early 1996 when a dispute flared concerning
sovereignty of a rocky offshore islet and troops for both
sides were rapidly mobilized. During the Nato Summit
in 1997, mediation attempts of US Foreign Minister
Albright succeeded in an agreement between Simitis and
Demirel to resolve existant conflicts peacefully.

The Infrastructure

On the mainland and the larger islands there is a good **road
system**. Away from a capital, roads on smaller islands can
rapidly degenerate to a paved (or rough), single track road.
Public transport is often unpredictable; some villages
served by a bus a day. The **ports** are busy centres for the
ferry system – the main commercial link for all the islands.
Key islands in all groups are connected with Athens
(Piraeus) and a handful of other mainland ports: others can
then be reached by **ferry boat** and **hydrofoil** connections.

WOMEN'S AGRICULTURAL COOP

Traditionally, women in rural
or agricultural areas have
worked physically very hard
on the land: sowing, reaping,
harvesting olives, picking
grapes, tending to livestock
and still rearing children and
doing housework. European
women have largely become
emancipated by industrial
mechanization, but in the
Greek Isles subsistence
farming remains. To facilitate
economic independence and
intellectual acualization of
women, the **Greek Council
for Equality** launched the
Women's Agricultural
Cooperatives in 1985. The
cooperatives attract tourists
who want to experience
Greek farming and village life
and who pay to work there.
The organization and running
is the responsibility of the
women thus enabling them
to acquire managerial skills
and independence.

Zeus disguised himself as a
white bull and carried off
Europa who later bore him
three sons: **Rhadamanthys**,
Minos and **Sarpedon**.
Pasiphaë, wife of **Minos**, fell
in love with a bull from the
sea sent by **Poseidon** – their
unfortunate union resulted in
the **Minotaur** (head of a bull
on a man's body) whom
Minos hid in a labyrinth under
his palace. Minos was sent
seven maidens and seven
youths every nine years from
Athens as compensation for
the death of his son during
an Athenian game. Minos fed
the Minotaur the blood of his
victims. **Theseus**, son of the
king of Athens, wanted to end
this cruel practice, so third
time round he also went. With
the help of **Ariadne**, daughter
of Minos, and a long thread,
he entered the Labyrinth and
slew the Minotaus.

THE PEOPLE

Travelling for trade has been a necessity for many
Greeks, not only between islands and the mainland but
much further afield. Large numbers of people of Greek
origin live in the USA, UK, Australia and South Africa
and inevitably they become involved in commerce of
some sort. But wherever they end up, Greeks have an
undying affection for their natal island. Each island has a
distinct character and there are intense rivalries between
islanders involving niggling issues which go back to
Classical times – usually the source of good-natured
banter rather than the blood feuds associated with the
Maniots in the Peloponnese.

Family Life

Island Greeks are extremely friendly people – the word
for stranger and friend – *xenós* – is the same. Greek
males often make a play for foreign female visitors –
the practice is called *kamákia* (harpoon, fishing trident).
This game of point scoring is not played by all, however,
and is scorned on by many Greeks. Some visitors may
welcome the attention – if it's unwanted, it simply pays
to be polite but very firm.

Newspapers outside Greece have been quick to warn of an increase in reported rapes of female tourists – a phenomenon virtually unknown within Greek culture. For a foreign male to become seriously involved with a Greek girl still creates opposition even in the most enlightened families. Greeks have a deep and genuine love of children as visitors with families quickly find out – Greek children, especially sons, are indulged.

Religion

Religion has always had a focal position within Greek cultures ever since the first Greeks from Central Asia brought with them the worship of a **mother goddess**. **Christianity** was adopted in Roman times during the rule of the Emperor Constantine. The Old and New Testaments written in Greek in the 4th century AD are in use today by the **Greek Orthodox Church**, to which 98% of the population belongs. Superficially, many Greeks might appear to have moved away from the church – until births, deaths and marriages bring them back. Most people get married in church, sceptics included, although Papandreou legalized civil marriages. Within island communities the role of the church is central and the priest carries great respect within a community. Small **Catholic** populations still exist in the Cyclades – a remnant of Latin rule.

Greeks revere their places of worship and, whatever a visitor's views on religion, offence is avoided if they enter modestly dressed. Convention still dictates that widows wear black for several years following the death of a husband or other loved ones – men get away lightly since widowers are only required to wear a black armband for a year.

Tradition dictated that each family built its own chapel – hence the plethora of tiny chapels on the islands. In Athens and some island towns there are traces of the Ottoman (Turkish) occupation and **minarets** are visible on the skyline of towns in the Aegean islands though the **mosques** beneath tend to be used as museums and not for worship.

Opposite: *For religious festivals traditional dress and customs are preserved.* **Below:** *Greek priests are a familiar aspect of Greek life.*

Myths and Legends

The Greek people retain a strong sense of their past, whether through recorded history or legends. Every island (conscious of the tourist potential) makes great play of its links with the mythical gods and goddesses of the ancient world and tales of their rivalries, affairs and involvement with humans have fascinated people for centuries. The early Greeks were ingenious in incorporating deities into the pantheon of Greek gods and the Romans essentially retained them under different names.

In the beginning . . .was **Chaos**: from Chaos emerged **Gaia** (mother earth) who gave birth to a son, **Uranus** (Ouranos – Sky). The union of mother and her son produced an unholy brood which included the **Titans** and the one-eyed giants, the **Cyclops**. Gaia finally gave birth to a **Golden Race** who lived in a world without trouble or wars: they died out, childless, but their spirits lingered on earth.

Kronos, leader of the Titans, married his sister **Rhea**. It had been prophesied that Kronos would be killed by the hand of one of his own children, so he ate them one by one as they were born. Rhea's sixth child was **Zeus** and she prepared to save him from a similar fate to those of his siblings by giving Kronos a stone to eat. She took Zeus away and he grew to manhood, hidden

from his father. He then returned to fulfil the prophecy by poisoning his father. Kronos coughed up, unharmed and now full-grown, all the children he had eaten, – **Pluto** and **Poseidon**, brothers of **Zeus** and sisters **Hestia**, **Demeter** and **Hera**. They became the main gods of Olympos.

Left: *Bouzoúki music can be enjoyed throughout the islands – the nimbleness of the fingers of the best players will surprise any guitarist.*
Opposite: *Brightly dressed Corfiot dancers perform traditional routines for visitors.*

Music

The real music of the Aegean lies behind the *bouzoúki*-dominated façade exemplified by the films *Never on a Sunday* (1959) and *Zorba the Greek* (1964). The melodies have haunting cadences; the rhythms and time signatures are almost hypnotic. Music was an essential element of Classical Greece, with a purity derived from simple five tone scales without harmonies. Middle Eastern (Ottoman and Arab) and Byzantine music later developed this. For the Greeks music has never been something separate from the people and their emotions. Greek rhythms, alien to lovers of mainstream classical or, indeed, rock music are certainly familiar to the jazz fan or reader of Homeric verse: 5/8, 7/8, 9/8 and 11/8 timings are intuitive to a Greek musician.

Among popular musicians, **Nana Mouskouri**, **Demis Roussos** and **John Vangelis** have all won considerable success on the international arena.

Dance

At festivals and weddings the dancing is very different from the contrived displays. The secret is *kéfi*, the Greek equivalent of 'soul', where the spirit moves the dancer and the improvised steps provide the lead for others.

ISLAND MUSIC

The Italian influence is unmistakeable in the music of the Ionian isles where much more 'western' melodies are played on guitar and violin. In Crete, Kárpathos, Chálki and Kássos the music has a distinctive sound due to the use of the *lyra* – a three-stringed fiddle balanced on the knee and accompanied by the *laoúta*, a lute-like instrument similar to the *oud* of Turkish and Arab music. In Kárpathos a primitive bagpipe (*tsamboúna* or *askómandra*) is played and in the Cyclades and most Aegean Islands the *lyra* is replaced by the *violi* (violin).

In Crete *pedektó* are very energetic dances with rapid steps while *sírto* embraces slower, almost shuffling dances. The national dance (*kalamatianó*) is a 12-step *sírto* in which a leader improvises and the rest of the dancers – hands joined and held at shoulder level – follow the leader's steps.

Zorba's dance derives from the *hasápiko* (called the butcher's dance) while *sírtáki*, usually performed by two or three men, is another energetic dance.

Above: *Greek statues, even when headless such as these at Délos, have an elegance of line.*

Writers and Poets

Many of the Greek myths can be traced back to the Mycenaean period and even earlier, thanks to **Homer's** *Illiad* and *Odyssey* in which he wrote down the stories belonging to an oral tradition already then approximately 500 years old.

The Homeric tradition influenced countless thousands in Greece and the west as part of a 'Classical education'. The comedies of **Aristophanes** have a mixture of cleverness and unashamed vulgarity which certainly appeals to modern audiences. And Shakespeare drew heavily on this classical legacy with numerous allusions to Greek history and mythology.

Modern Greek authors have gained renown but none more than the Cretan **Nikos Kazantzakis** who penned *Zorba the Greek, Christ Re-crucified, The Fratricides, Report to Greco* and *Freedom or Death*.

Poetry is alive and well in modern Greece with a tradition of intense and dynamic work: remarkably the country can boast two recent Nobel Laureates: **George Seferis** and **Odysseus Elytis**.

Crafts and Customs

Many people feel that the classic form of Greek sculpture has never been bettered and the same is felt by many about classical architecture. The creative energies of the greatest artists of the Byzantine era were devoted to a celebration of the Christian religion in icons and wall paintings. The best known of all Greek painters is **Domenico Theotokopoulos – El Greco**. Born in Crete in 1547, he studied under Titian in Venice and then settled in Toledo, Spain.

Traditional crafts such as embroidery, lace-making and pottery are thriving on the islands where a ready market is found with those visitors who want quality more than cheap souvenirs.

Sports and Recreation

For Greeks, the sport which really excites national emotions is **football**. Every small town will have its own football team commanding passionate (and often politically-oriented) support from locals. Every Greek male would claim to support one of the major-league teams (mostly based on the mainland) and for European Cup matches cafés are full of vocal supporters offering advice to hapless referees hampered by impaired vision…

REMBETIKA

Rembétika – reputedly the *bouzoúki* music of dens of iniquity where the women were fast and the smell of hashish hung on the air – began as music of the dispossessed. Prevalent themes were of death, oppression and drug addiction – Greek 'blues'. Much of the music was improvised and played on the Turkish *baglamá* – a forerunner of the *bouzoúki*. The Junta gave an unintended boost to Rembétika by banning it – young people examined the forbidden fruit and recognized the scent of rebellion.

OUT OF SEASON

Henry Miller, Lawrence Durrell and many other writers have travelled to the islands to complete a 'great work'. Whereas larger islands such as Crete and Rhodes can cater for tourists all the year round, small islands literally close shop during the winter months. But if you stay at this time and manage a few words of Greek you are welcomed as a traveller rather than tourist – Greeks are marvellous at spotting the difference.

Left: *Greek jewellery, often made to traditional designs, is obtainable on all larger islands.*

The effects of the inflow of water through the Strait of Gibraltar – with a higher nutrient level – tend to make fishing catches higher in the Ionian islands than the Aegean. In spring and summer, days can be almost windless around the western islands allowing fishermen to make susbstantial catches of **swordfish**, **tunny**, both red and grey **mullet**, **sea bass**, **squid**, **octopus** and the Mediterranean **lobster** (*astakós*). Unfortunately, overfishing has reduced catches in the past decade, making fish comparatively expensive.

Below: *Traditional cafés abound on islands. Visitors are welcome to sit down and watch the world go by over a cup of coffee.*

In schools, **handball** and **basketball** are popular sports and physical exercise is an important part of the curriculum. For visitors as well as for increasing numbers of Greeks one attraction is the range of water sports from **snorkelling** and **diving** to **water skiing**, **windsurfing** and even **parascending**. The rich have long continued the national love affair with boats through **private yachts** and **power boats**. For visitors facilities are always available throughout the island's larger resorts and upmarket hotels.

The *kafeneíon*, that male-dominated feature of Greek life, is an important part of island culture – here, men sit solving the problems of the day, drinking endless cups of coffee to a background clicking of their **worry beads** or the pieces on a *tavoli* (backgammon) board. Traditional Greek coffee is a finely ground mocha boiled in a pot and served in a small cup. *Kafés glykós* is for those with a sweet tooth, *métrios* is medium and *skétos* unsweetened. A glass of cold water is served with coffee – beware the coffee is unfiltered and the grounds are in the bottom of the cup. Locals are used to seeing foreign females in cafés but still take a very dim view of any Greek women behaving so 'outrageously'.

Food and Drink

To sample really good Greek food, try waiting and watching where the local Greeks go.

Estiatórias often serve a variety of casserole dishes: *moussakas* (originally lamb with plenty of aubergine – not the beef and mashed potato tourist version) or *pastíccio* – similar, with pasta rather than potato, all selected by going into the kitchen and choosing from the pots of food. **Tavernas** range from the grass-roofed beach variety to the specialist **Psárotaverna** (fish) and **Psistaría** (spit-roast meats). They serve a selection of *hors d'oeuvres* (*mezédhes*) with a main course of fish or meat (grilled or fried), *patátes* (chips) and the ubiquitous Greek salad (*khoriátiki saláta*) of coarse-chopped tomatoes, cucumber, onion and peppers topped with féta cheese, olives and a dribble of olive oil.

Starters include *taramasaláta* (made with smoked cod's roe), *tzatzíki* (yoghurt with garlic, cucumber and mint), *eliés* (green or black olives) – try the excellent *kalamata* variety with a pointed end, *rossikisaláta* (potato salad with mayonnaise), *yigándes* (haricot beans in tomato sauce or vinaigrette), *kolokithákia* (deep-fried courgette) served with *skordhália* (a simple

Above: *For Greeks eating is a leisurely activity with numerous small dishes, friends and conversation.*

CRETAN FARE

Mountain honey and cheeses from Crete were famed throughout the ancient world:
Myzithra • soft, white and ricotta-like cheese.
Ladótiro • white cheese in olive oil.
Stáka • rich white cheese, often baked in a pie.
Traditional pastries include:
Xerotigana • a pancake filled with honey and nuts.
Amygdalópitta • a sweet almond pie.
Kaltzoúni • tartlets with a sweet syrup filling.
Raki • Cretan moonshine, distilled in the mountains.

garlic sauce), *mavromatiká*
(black-eyed beans), *saganáki*
(fried cheese) and *tiropitta* or
spanachópitta (small pasties of
cheese or spinach respectively).

Vegetarians should check
that mince meat has not been
added to the rice when ordering
yemístes (stuffed vegetables) or
dolmádhes (stuffed vine-leaves),
and even vegetable soups will
be made with chicken stock.
With the influx of young foreigners the idea of not eating
meat through choice is accepted though totally alien: the
Greek word for vegetarian is
hortofágos (grass eater) – which
says it all. Fish tends to be
expensive everywhere in
Greece because catches are

Above: *Fish, although
expensive, is a favourite
with visitors. Smaller island
restaurants catch their own
– you dine on the freshest
fish imaginable.*

smaller due to over-fishing. Worth trying are: *barboúnia*
(grilled red mullet), *marídhes* (fried whitebait) and *xifía*
(swordfish marinated in oil and lemon and grilled). *Kala-
marákia* (deep-fried squid) are excellent when freshly
caught, but most restaurant fare comes frozen from the
Far East. *Astakós* (lobster) is particularly good in the
Ionian Islands: *garidhes* (shrimps or prawns) are always
expensive. Meat dishes include *keftédhes* (meatballs),
biftékia (a sort of rissole-cum-hamburger), *souvlákia*
(grilled kebabs), *arni psitó* (roast lamb) and *katsíki* (roast
kid). Local Greek fruit is excellent in season with oranges,
lemons, apples, pears, apricots, peaches, nectarines,
grapes, figs, melons and pomegranates fresh off the tree.

Greeks have a very sweet tooth and buy cakes and
pastries from a **zacharoplastía** (patisserie-cum-café)
rather than at a restaurant. Desserts include *baklavá* (a
nut-filled puff pastry soaked in sugar syrup, and *kataifi*
(chopped walnuts and honey wrapped in shredded
wheat). The **galaktopolía** sell dairy products including

WHERE TO EAT

On the more popular islands,
fast-food outlets are well
established. Although mainly
drinking establishments,
oúzeries also serve snacks
(*mezédhes*); street stands
called girós serve sandwiches
(*híro*) and kebab (*souvlákia*)
either to take away or eat
at a few tables. Estiatória are
usually more up-market places
than the ubiquitous tavernas.

kréma (custard), *rizógalo* (rice pudding) and locally made *yiaoúrti* (yoghurt – the best is made from ewe's milk). Try the zacharoplastía and galaktopolía for a far better continental breakfast than the regulation fare in hotels. Honey, usually of the very runny kind, is a great favourite and often served poured over creamy, fresh yoghurt. Useful lunchtime or picnic stand-by's are the larger versions of the pasties mentioned above made with filo pastry: *tiropitta*, filled with minted cheese, *spanachópitta* with spinach and cheese or, *eliópitta* with black olives. *Féta* is the best known Greek cheese – if buying loose, ask to try a bit since some can be very salty: *graviéra* is a locally-made Gruyére-type cheese.

Drinks

Many foreign **beers** are made in Greece under licence; they are cheaper by the bottle than canned. **Oúzo**, the aniseed-based spirit, is synonymous with Greek holidays. It is served with iced water which is tipped into the oúzo turning it milky-white – the smoothest brands come from Sámos and Lésbos. Greek **brandies** – the best known is *Metáxas* – are heavier and rougher than their French counterparts but very good as the base of drinks such as brandy sour or Alexander. Greece was famed for its **wine** in antiquity but whereas Bulgaria and Hungary have been quick to use Australian expertise to revolutionize their wines, the same is only just beginning to happen in Greece. Nevertheless, Greek wines drunk on their home ground are perfectly acceptable although you may find that they do not 'travel' and are better as a holiday memory. Every tourist resort has shops selling sundry, locally produced 'liqueurs'.

Below: *Oúzo is traditionally served with* mezédhes. *Genuine oúzeries are hard to find but worth the effort.*

2
Athens

The Greek capital is usually the starting point for ferry journeys for independent travellers and can be a visitor's first real contact with Greece.

It was inevitable that a settlement would grow where modern Athens is sited today since the location offered early settlers (3500BC) unimpeded views to the sea, protection from a ring of mountains, and a natural spring. The **Mycenaeans** established the first walled palace-fortress, the **Acropolis**, in 1300BC.

Initial impressions of Athens are coloured by its size, noise, ceaseless bustle and barely breathable air. This is a city of around 3,000,000 inhabitants – a third of the entire population of Greece – with about the same number again passing through as visitors each year. Athens can be intimidating until you have found a place to stay and had time to wander. Not far from the hurly-burly lies the **Pláka** district just below the **Acropolis** with its innumerable family-run tavernas and small parks. The city is famed for its incomparable ancient monuments – the **Parthenon** and the **Temple of Athena Nike** (*Wingless Victory*) sit on the Acropolis and in the surrounding city are temples, theatres and one of the finest museums in the world. Athenians think affectionately of their city as the country's largest village. Its smog (*néfos*) is another question. A million or more cars choke the narrow streets of Athens and their exhaust gases in turn asphyxiate the inhabitants. On some days a brown pall hangs threateningly over Athens drawing unflattering comparison with Mexico City – the most polluted city in the world.

ATHENS

DON'T MISS

*** **Acropolis:** surmounted by the Parthenon – the world's best known temple.
*** **Temple of Athena Nike:** the smaller but elegant challenger to the Parthenon on the Acropolis.
*** **Pláka:** the lively area below the Acropolis filled with a variety of restaurants, cafés and shops.
** **National Archaeological Museum:** a veritable treasure house of Greek history.
* **Erechtheion:** with statues of the Caryatids.

Opposite: *The Parthenon symbolizes the glory of Classical Greece and makes a memorable spectacle.*

CITY SIGHTSEEING
The Squares *

Athens is an easy city to explore – whether you stay
centrally or travel into the centre by bus or taxi, everyone
can direct you back to **Sýntagma Square** (Constitution
Square), packed with airline offices and overpriced cafés.
Omónia Square, another landmark to the northwest of
Sýntagma, has little to commend it, but **Pláka** is a maze of
small streets crammed with souvenir shops, bars and
restaurants at the foot of the Acropolis. The colourful flea
market to the west of **Monastiráki Square** lies close to
Pláka (and the metro station). Behind the national museum
lies **Exarchía Square** – a lively yet relaxed place and
home of poets and the free-spirited.

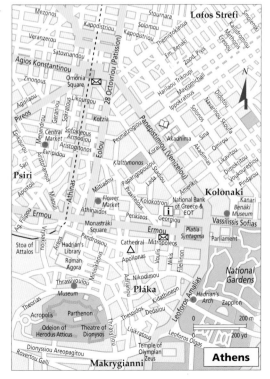

The Acropolis ***

In general, the name given
to any stony, fortified hill
on which a temple was
built at the centre of
a town, is today associated
throughout the world with
the craggy, limestone hill
rising 100m (328ft) above
the **Plain of Attica** around
which Athens grew. The
city had been sacked and
devastated by a Persian
invasion so in about 450BC
Pericles, the ruler of
Athens during that time,
decided to rebuild the
temples of the Acropolis
(*akros* = topmost, *polis* =
city). To this end he expro-
priated most of the funds
intended for the protection
of the islands that formed
part of the Délian League
with Athens (*see* p. 14).

The Parthenon ✦✦✦

No temple is better known than the **Parthenon** with its 46 Doric columns in an outer colonnade epitomizing Classical Greek architecture. It was built under the direction of the gifted sculptor Phidias between 447 and 432BC of white marble brought from quarries on Mt Pendéli northeast of the city. Inside was Phidias' 11m-high (36ft) statue of **Athena Parthénos** crafted in gold and ivory. Its architects and builders curved foundations and bent columns inwards with extraordinary precision to create the illusion of straight lines and the desired perspective. Even the approach via the **Propylaia** (monumental gateway) grants a carefully calculated three-quarter view of the temple. A Doric frieze (now incomplete) once surmounted the columns and there was a roof until 1687 when a Venetian 'bomb' hit the Turkish powder stores inside.

Corrosion of the marble by the smog was in danger of destroying the columns and carvings and past attempts at restoration had been unsatisfactory. A remarkable reconstruction job is still underway using titanium rods to strengthen columns and epoxy resins to reduce the porosity of the damaged marble.

Above: *Female statues, the Caryatids, take the place of ornate columns in supporting the roof of the porch in front of the Erechtheion.*
Below: *Bustling Pláka, a maze of streets, small shops, cafés and restaurants in what remains of Medieval Athens.*

The Temple of Athena Nike ✦✦✦

Built by **Kallikrates** after the Parthenon (420BC) but from the same pentelic marble on the site of an older shrine to the goddess. The temple is also known as *Wingless Victory* – it once housed a statue of Athena in gold and ivory some 12m (39ft) tall.

Below: *The Odeon of
Hérodus Atticus (AD161)
is the focus of the annual
Festival of Athens and a
venue for theatre, ballet
and classical music.*
Opposite: *The frieze on
the Tower of Winds depicts
the eight winds – one on
each of its sides.*

The Erechtheion ★★

The Erechtheion, a sanctuary of Athena, is an unusual
building with three porches built over the much earlier
Mycenaean House of Erechtheus. According to mythology
the sacred olive tree created by Athena grew here and the
rock struck by Poseidon was close by. The temple was built
during the Periclean age (421BC), was later converted to a
Christian church and then became a harem for the
Ottoman Turks. Its fame comes from the six Caryatids –
the statues of maidens – which supported the roof: one of
these was removed by Elgin to the British Museum and
the remaining five are in the **Acropolis Museum**. The
Greek authorities have equipped the museum with air
filters to remove the corrosive component from the
Athens air and thus protect the artefacts displayed there.
Open daily 08:00–18:45; weekends 08:30–14:30.

Around the Acropolis ★★

The **Areópagus** which is the hill of Ares, God of War, lies
to the west of the Acropolis just below the entrance. The
city's High Council sat here and the nearby hill of the Pnyx
was the meeting place for the democratic assembly. Two
ancient theatres are built into the hill on its south side,
accessible from Dhionision Areopayito. The **Theatre of
Hérodus Atticus** is named after the second century philan-

thropist whose riches
funded it – performances
are still given during the
Festival of Athens (mid-
May and September). **The
Theatre of Diónysos** was
built in the 6th century BC –
parts of the theatre are decorated with frescoes based
on the life of Dionysos dating from the 1st century AD
(open daily 08:30–14:30).
Above the theatre is an
Asklepeion – sanctuary to
Asklepios, god of healing.

The ancient **Agorá** (market place) or forum on the western edge of Pláka is a confused jumble of ruins spanning its long life as the city's market place – from 6th century BC to the 5th century AD (open Tuesday–Sunday 08:00–14:30). The **Theseum** to the west of the Agorá is a Doric temple dedicated to Hephaistos – god of

blacksmiths and metal workers – and was the first building in Pericles' reconstruction of the city. Between the ancient Agorá and Acropolis lies the **Roman Agorá** which was built as an extension to the old Agorá by the Caesars Julius and Augustus (open Tuesday–Sunday 08:00– 14:30). The intriguing **Aéridhes** (Tower of the Winds) at the eastern edge of the Roman Agorá is an octagonal observatory building designed by a Syrian astronomer which functioned as compass, sundial, weather vane and water clock. Originally **Hadrian's Library** (situated north of the Roman Agorá) included a court with 100 columns but now only large walls survive to show its former extent.

PLACES OF INTEREST

Keramikós, the ancient cemetery about 1km (⅔ miles) northwest of the Acropolis was used for burials well into Roman times. There are some remarkable tombs of rich Athenians from the 4th and 5th centuries BC resembling miniature temples or sphinxes: more modest are the large stone-carved vases indicating the resting places of the unmarried dead. It is a quiet place with a stream, resident tortoises and a surprising number of species of wild flowers (open Tuesday–Sunday 08:00–14:30).

To the east of the Acropolis lies the **Monument of Lysikrátes** built in 335BC where six Corinthian columns support a marble dome, surprisingly still intact. Across the busy Leofóros Amalías Avenue leading to Platía Sýntagma stand 15 enormous pillars marking the **Temple of Olympian Zeus** (open Tuesday–Sunday

---

SHOPPING

Try the Sunday morning flea markets held in **Monastiráki**, **Thission** and **Piraeus**. **Pláka** also has an abundance of shops geared to the tourist trade. Street markets (*laikí agorá*) run in various Athenian neighbourhoods on different days of the week and sell a wide range of household goods and foodstuffs.

The main museums (**Benáki**, **Cycladic Art** and **National Archaeological**) have shops with high-quality reproductions and original art on sale. For antiques, there is a collection of shops on **Adhrianoú**.

WOLF MOUNTAIN

It is a long time since the four-footed genuine creatures howled on **Lykavittos** – Wolf Mountain. From **Kolonáki Square** – patronized by the wealthy – it is a long climb on foot but a funicular railway takes you up to the **Chapel of St George**. From up here is a superb view over Athens and Piraeus, atmospheric clarity permitting.

Above: *The Temple of Poseidon sits high above the sea at Sounion, south of Athens – a landmark for passing ships.*

08:00–14:30) – nearby **Hadrian's Arch** marks the boundary between the classical city and the one Hadrian built. Beyond the temple and extending east and north to the **Parliament** buildings lies the extensive area of the **National Gardens**. Not for the lovers of well-kept formal gardens, this unkempt area of trees and shrubs is a lung for the city and a lovely place to wander in spring among the flowers, trees and birds.

MUSEUMS

Modern display techniques might not yet have reached the **Greek National Archaeological Museum** but no museum in the world can possibly draw on a richer heritage. Among its many treasures are the golden mask of Agamemnon in the Mycenaean hall, the sculpture of a Cycladic man playing a lyre and the wonderful, Classical statue of Poseidon discovered in the sea just off Evia (1 Tossitsa Street, open Tuesday–Sunday 08:00–19:00; Monday 12:00–19:00).

The **Benáki Museum** houses the superb personal acquisitions of Emmanuel Benáki drawn from the Byzantine and Islamic world (22 Vas. Sophías Avenue). Unfortunately the museum is closed to the public but is scheduled to re-open sometime in the future.

The ground floor of the **Byzantine Museum** consists of three separate chapels: early Christian, middle Byzantine and after (Vas Sophias Avenue. Open Tuesday–Sunday 08:30–15:00). The **Museum of Cycladic Art** lies between the Byzantine and Benáki museums and contains a remarkable collection of Cycladic figurines dating from 3200BC onwards. Open 10:00–16:00; Saturday 10:00–14:30; closed Tuesday and Sunday.

Sounion **

An easy day trip from Athens is to the 5th-century **Temple of Poseidon** at Sounion, whose columns form an imposing landmark. Organized trips to Sounion are advertised from every travel outlet around Sýntagma Square – regular buses leave from the KTEL terminal to the southwest of Aréos park. In summer it is crowded, particularly towards evening – for views of the sunset.

PIRAEUS

Piraeus, the main port of Greece in Classical times, was once linked to the city of Athens by long walls. Today, Piraeus is as busy as any port in the Mediterranean because Greece is still a maritime nation and a high proportion of the merchant shipping is owned by a few distinguished and well-known Greek families.

The best antidote to its busy streets and concrete buildings is to escape and go into Athens via the **metro** (*elektrikó*) with convenient city-centre stations at Omónia, Monastírion and Theseíon buses (no. 040) run day and night to Sýntagma. There are two museums based in Piraeus. The **Archaeological Museum** at 31 Har. Trokoúpi Street has a good collection of exhibits (open Tuesday–Sunday 08:00–14:30) and the **Maritime Museum** on Akti Themistoclés by Freatídos Street has collections of models and memorabilia dedicated to the glory of Greece in its various maritime battles (open Tuesday–Friday 09:00–14:00, Saturday–Sunday 09:00–13:00). Excellent **marinas** are also found further along the coast at **Vouliagméni** and **Glyfáda**.

> ### A HAVEN
>
> A taxi or bus (no. 224) from Akadhimias leading from the northwest corner of Sýntagma can take you to the suburb of Kaisariani and a half-hour walk to the **Byzantine monastery** at the foot of **Mt Hymettus**. Just beyond the monastery, paths lead under pine trees on to the slopes of Hymettus, which in spring becomes a haven for over 20 species of wild orchid, a bewildering array of other plants, tortoises and singing birds. On a clear day a tiny, white Parthenon is visible from here, far below on the distant Acropolis.

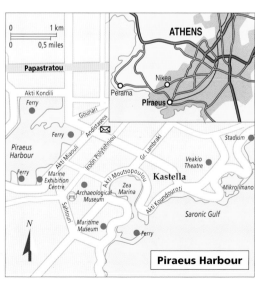

Piraeus Harbour

Athens and Piraeus at a Glance

BEST TIMES TO VISIT

In **Spring**, March–May, the light shows the ruins at their best, wildflowers are in bloom and the weather is warm. In **Summer**, June–September, Athens can be dusty and smog a problem during the day – evenings are cooler and the Athens Festival hosts various music concerts in the city. **Winter** months, November to January, can be cold but October is warm and clear.

GETTING THERE

Direct **flights** daily to Athens from London, New York and European destinations. All international and charter flights arrive at **Ellinikón Airport East terminal**, with the exception of Olympic Airways flights which arrive at **West terminal**, known as **Olympiki.** During the summer charter flights operate from many UK, European and North American capitals to **Athens** and also direct to some islands. Surplus charter flights are advertised in newspapers and sold cheaply. It can be cheaper for visitors from North America to book a flight to London and pick up a charter flight to Athens. **Olympic Airways** has reduced Superapex fares from London, and **island or inter-island connections** can be booked at the same time. Ferries from Italy are mostly from **Ancona**, **Bari**, **Brindisi**, **Otranto** and **Venice**, which connect with **Corfu** and then **Patrás**. From

here, there is transfer by road to Athens. The **Brindisi** ferry connects with the train from Rome.There are no direct trains from London to Athens. The most direct route is through **Italy** via **Paris** and **Bologna** to **Brindisi** and then to take the ferry to **Patrás**. **British Rail International**, tel: (0171) 834-2345 will be able to give you current information.

GETTING AROUND

Blue and yellow double decker **airport buses** run from Amalías Avenue (Sýntagma Square) every 20 minutes between 06:00–23:30 and through the night at roughly hourly intervals (00:40, 01:59, 02:50, 04:00 and 05:00) with pick-ups at Omónia Square. Bus #091 for East terminal and bus #091 for West terminal. Buses from **Piraeus** (#19) serve **both** airports. Athens is well served by **city buses**. Different areas of the mainland have separate bus terminals, some also serving islands: to reach the terminal at 100 **Kifissoú Street**, take **bus #51** from Omónia Square. Connections from terminal to Corfu, Kefalonía, Lefkada and Patrás for Ionian isles. To reach the terminal at 260 **Liossion Street**, take **bus #24** from Leofóros Amalías in city. Connections from terminal to Evia – both Chálki and Loútra – and Vólos for Sporades. To reach **Mavromatéon** terminal, take **tram 5** or **9**

towards Areos Park on 28 Octovriou Street. Connections from terminal to Rafína which serve Evia and the Cyclades. **Taxis** in Athens are cheap and reliable and an underground rail system, **Metro** (*Elektriko*), runs from Piraeus to Kifissía via Thissío, Monastiráki, Omónia, and Plateia Viktorias. To be extended to Sýntagma Square. (*See* page124 for on-line timetable and bookings.)

WHERE TO STAY

Athens
LUXURY
Grande Bretagne, Sýntagma Square, Athens, tel: (01) 333-0000, fax: (01) 322-8034. Elegant rooms, marble lobby – grandeur from a bygone age. **N.J.V. Meridian**, 2 Vass. Geórgiou, tel: (01) 325-5301, fax: (01) 323-5856. Modern and comfortable. **Royal Olympic Hotel**, 28 Diákou, tel: (01) 922-6411, fax: (01) 923-3317. American style overlooking Temple of Zeus and Lykavittos. **Pentelikon**, 66 Diligiánni Street, Kefalári, tel: (01) 623-0650, fax (01) 801-0314. An elegant, old hotel with a lovely garden in Kifissia. **The Elektra Palace**, 18 Nikodímou St., tel: (01) 324-1401, fax: (01) 324-1875. Smart hotel, rooftop swimming pool and Pláka close-by. **Airotel Parthenon**, 6 Makrí St., tel: (01) 923-4594, fax: (01) 921-5569. Outdoor breakfast garden. Near Hadrian's Gate.

MID-RANGE

Adams Hotel, Herefóntos and Thálou, tel: (01) 324-6582, fax: (01) 323-8533. Comfortable pension, near Hadrian's Arch.
Hotel Hermes, 19 Apollónos, tel: (01) 323-5514, fax: (01) 323-2073. Views of Acropolis.
Akropol, 71 Pentelis Avenue, tel: (01) 682-6650, fax: (01) 684-5057. Popular with business visitors. Pleasant garden.

BUDGET

Pension Adonis, 3 Kódrou, tel: (01) 324-9737, fax: (01) 323-1062 Excellent value, very clean. Good views.
Akropolis House, 6–8 Kódrou, tel: (01) 322-3244, fax: (01) 324-4143. Traditional pension with antique furniture.

Piraeus
MID-RANGE

Hotel Anemoni, Karaóli Demetríou and Evripídou, tel: (01) 411-1768, fax: (01) 411-1743. Quiet and clean.
The Lilia, 131 Zéas, Passalimáni, tel: (01) 417-9108, fax: (01) 411-4311. Clean and with a courtesy bus to the port.

BUDGET

Ionian Family Hotel, 10 Kapodistríou, tel: (01) 417-7537. Basic but convenient.

WHERE TO EAT

Pláka
Thespes, 18 Thespídou, tel: (01) 323-8243. Rooftop taverna with good food and plenty of character.

Platanos, 4 Diogénis, tel: (01) 322-0666. Unpretentious but very good food.
Byzantino, 18 Kidathinéon, tel: (01) 322-7368. Tables under trees: excellent value.
Xynou Taverna, 4 Angeloú Gerontá Street, tel: (01) 322-1065. Traditional, fine food.
Eden, 12 Lissíou and Mnissikléous, tel: (01) 324-8858 – good vegetarian mousakkas and quiches.

Around Pláka
Daphne's, 4 Lysikrátous, tel: (01) 322-7971. Greek and international cuisine.
Kouvelos, 5 Lembéssi St., tel: (01) 922-1183. Near Hadrian's Arch, specializes in mezédhes.
Socrates Prison, 20 Mitséon, tel: (01) 922-3434. Very popular with locals, Greek cuisine with a more adventurous air.

Exárchia and Koukáki (near the Archaeological Museum). Embraces the area where food is good and reasonably priced.
To Meltemi, 26 Zínni, Koukáki. A genuine oúzerie, excellent seafood mezédhes.
I Gardenia, 29 Zinni, Koukáki. Cheap, traditional casserole dishes. Wine from the barrel.

TOURS AND EXCURSIONS

Around Sýntagma Square and Pláka there are many travel agents offering trips to the major Greek sites. These include **Delphi**, **Corinth** and then further afield into the Peloponnese for **Epidavros**, **Mycenae** and **Olympia**. One of the easiest trips to make is to **Sounion**, south of Athens, and the magnificent **Temple of Poseidon** – either by regular service coach from KTEL terminal (Areos Square) or organized trips (travel agents).

USEFUL CONTACTS

Tourist Police: Akti Miaolou, tel: (01) 924-3354.
Emergency number in Athens, tel: 171.
Ambulance, tel: 166.
ELPA (Greek Automobile Association), tel: 104.
EOT or **NTOG (National Tourist Organization of Greece)**, 2 Ameríkis Street 10564, tel: (01) 322-3111/9, fax: (01) 322-4148.
East Airport terminal, tel: (01) 969-9500.
EOT office inside National Bank of Greece, Sýntagma Square, 2 Karageórgi Servias Street, tel: (01) 325-2267/8.

ATHENS	J	F	M	A	M	J	J	A	S	O	N	D
AVERAGE TEMP. °F	48	49	54	60	68	76	82	82	76	66	58	52
AVERAGE TEMP. °C	11	11	12	16	20	25	28	28	25	19	15	12
HOURS OF SUN DAILY	5	5	7	9	11	15	12	11	9	6	5	4
RAINFALL ins.	2.12	1.81	1.26	0.8	0.74	0.47	0.16	0.32	0.63	1.73	2.48	2.84
RAINFALL mm	54	46	32	21	19	12	4	8	16	44	63	72
DAYS OF RAINFALL	11	11	10	9	8	5	3	4	4	8	11	11

3
Crete

Crete, the largest of the Greek islands, is almost a separate country. The island lies west to east, stretching for 277km (173 miles) with a massive mountainous spine soaring to over 2400m (7874ft) in places. Crete is riven north to south by deep gorges which divide the island into four main provinces (*nomós*). In the south the fertile **Messára plain** and to the east the **Lassíthi plateau** both provide a diversity of vegetables and fruit for local consumption and export to the rest of Greece.

The north coast of Crete, from **Haniá** (or Chaniá) to **Sitía**, has suffered most from the ravages of mass tourism but out of season Crete rapidly regains its dignity – flights and ferries run all year round. Spring begins early with anemones out at Christmas – in April Crete's wildflowers are a magnet for naturalists with the snow-capped white mountains providing a sumptuous backdrop. The island's extraordinary Minoan heritage makes **Knossós** the busiest archaeological site in Greece after the Acropolis. The **Archaeological Museum** in **Iráklion** where many Minoan finds are displayed is astonishing.

Cretans have valued their liberty above everything and, although German forces occupied the island in 1941, the islanders never faultered in their resistance. The theme of freedom has been carried far and wide by the island's famous sons – painter **El Greco**, diplomat and politician **Elefthérios Venizélos**, the author **Nikos Kazantzákis** and composer **Míkis Theodorákis**. Young people, in particular, are taking great pride in preserving the island's unique heritage of music and dance.

DON'T MISS

*** **Knossós:** remains of an ancient city including Minoan palace with Sir Arthur Evans' painted reconstructions.
*** **Iráklion Archaeology Museum:** an outstanding museum by any standards.
** **Samariá Gorge:** walk from mountains to the sea in Europe's longest gorge.
** **Phaistós and Ayia Triádha:** important archaeological site for Minoan grandeur in great scenery.

Opposite: *Knossós, most famous of the Minoan palaces, can still be relatively crowd free when visited in early morning or late evening.*

Below: *Reconstruction of Minoan frescoes on inner walls at Knossós.*

NORTH COAST

Nomós Irákliou ★★

Iráklion, the fifth largest city in Greece and the Cretan capital since 1971, was first established as the Minoan port of Knossós and later became the Saracen base for piracy and the slave trade. An exploration of old Iráklion can begin with the Venetian harbour : the **Lion of St Mark** guards the recently restored **Rocco al Mare**, a 16th-century fortress; the nearby arches of the **Venetian Arsenali** (the shipyards) are partially hidden by the street.

The busy main thoroughfare, 25 Avgoústou, leads away from the harbour towards the **Venetian Loggia** (a meeting place for the nobility) and the **Venetian Church of San Marco** (1239); the **Morosins Fountain** with its lions stands in Plateia Venizélou. By law, the **Archaeological Museum** near Plateía Eleftherías can claim every important artefact found on the island, thus its Minoan collections have no equal and it is definitely worth a visit.

The island of Dhía just off the coast offers a day's escape from Iráklion: the island is a reserve for **kri-kri** (*Agrimi*), the Cretan wild goat (*see* p. 10).

Knossós ★★★

Knossós, the second most visited site in Greece after the Acropolis, is served every 10 minutes by buses from the modern harbour. Visit as it opens or out of season to avoid crowds drawn by the fascinating but sometimes fanciful reconstructions by Sir Arthur Evans (1900–1920). Visitors can see remains of a magnificent **Minoan** palace, royal villa and caravanserai from the Neopalatial period (1700–1380BC). The city of Knossós housed a population of between 30,000 and 100,000; the last palace to be built apparently had over 1300 rooms and was perhaps the inspiration for the myth of the 'labyrinth' in which Theseus fought the Minotaur. Open daily 08:00–19:00 in summer and 08:00–17:00 in winter.

Nomós Lassíthiou – Eastern Crete ★★

Agios Nikólaos, now Crete's best-known harbour-resort, was once the harbour for the city of Lato. Krítsa has become the traditional Cretan village for day trips from Agios Nikólaos as its 13th-century church (Panayía Kerá) has superb Byzantine frescoes. North of Krítsa lies Lato, a 4km (2½ miles) drive, lying between two hills. The corniche road along the **Gulf of Mirabello** leads to **Sitía**, passing several noteworthy sites: **Vrondá**, a Minoan cemetery, and further on the lofty **Kástro** with superb views over the gulf. Sitía with its long, sandy beach has retained its soul compared with other resorts.

Above: Once a sleepy harbour, Agios Nikólaos is now a busy town.

WHITE MOUNTAINS

Entrance to the Samariá Gorge lies at the southern end of the Omalós Plateau. A fee is charged which provides for wildlife rangers before descent of the steep but well-kept Xilóskalo (wooden staircase). From the gorge entrance the walk to Agia Roúmeli takes five to eight hours depending on slopes and pace. The path passes the tiny chapel of Samariá and continues southwards to the coast through the Sideróportes ('Iron Gates') where the gorge narrows dramatically. There are several hotels at Agia Roúmeli reached only by ferries which operate to Paleochóra and Hóra Sfakion. Over 250,000 people visit annually but their route is restricted to the bottom of the gorge. Numerous flowers appear on the rock walls in spring.

The surrounding countryside has a wealth of archaeological sites. Vái, a tourist magnet, boasts a superb beach and grove of palm trees (*Phoenix theophrastus*) of a species unique to Crete. The fertile Lassíthi Plateau with its thousands of windmills (no longer with sails) can be reached by buses from Mália, Iráklion or Agios Nikólaos. From Psychro on the western edge of the plain, the climb begins to the Dhiktean cave – birthplace of Zeus and a shrine from Minoan times.

Above: *Réthimnon harbour retains a great deal of charm and some good fish restaurants.*

MINOAN CIVILIZATION

The Copper and Bronze Age Minoan civilization falls into distinct periods –
Pre-Palatial 2600–1900BC: sanctuaries built in high places, first monumental *tholos* tombs.
Old Palace Period 1900–1700BC: first plumbing, bull culture predominant, Crete dominated the seas, thalassocracy.
New Palace Period 1700–1450BC: elaborate re-building of palaces and fancy villas after devastating earthquake, art flourishes.
Post-Palace Period 1450: volcanic eruption hits Thíra (Santoríni).
1450–1100BC:: tidal waves and earthquakes hit Crete, gradual infiltration of the Mycenaean culture.

Nomós Réthimnon – Central Crete ★★

Réthimnon's delightful Venetian harbour is surrounded by fish restaurants and a pair of minarets add an eastern touch to the skyline – one above the **Nerandzes Mosque,** now a museum, (open daily 11:00–19:00, closed August) offers views over the old quarter. Near the harbour is the **Loggia**, built in 1600. Finest of the Venetian buildings, it is now the city library. The acropolis of ancient Réthimnon lies below the massive Venetian castle (**Fortezza**); the **Archaeological Museum** at its entrance was formerly a Turkish prison.

The huge bulk of snow-capped **Psilorítis** (Mt Idha) soars to 2452m (8058ft) some 25km (16 miles) southwest of Réthimnon. There are excellent walks (organized treks are advertised in Haniá) and the wild **Amári** valley on the southwest flank is a favourite with birdwatchers for its bearded vultures. **Arkádi Monastery**, set in wild country on the northern slopes, looks like a small fort .

Nomós Haniá – Western Crete ★★

Haniá, once the Turkish capital, is a great place to wander and find remnants of its **Venetian** and **Ottoman** buildings. Haniá's well-known covered market and harbour are popular with visitors. The impressively-domed **Mosque of the Janissaries** lies just off the harbour; **Kastélli**, the hill behind it, has been occupied since Neolithic times. The **White Mountains** (Lefká Ori) reach

2453m (8048ft) at **Mt Pachnés** and are cut by deep ravines – the most famous being the **Samariá Gorge** which, at 18km (11 miles), is the longest in Europe.

West of Haniá, the two peninsulas of Rhodópou and Gramvoússa are crowd free and scenically striking. A minor road leads off the main coast road as far as Afráta, last village on the **Rhodópou** peninsula, and a track leads for some 12km (7½ miles) towards the tip. Similarly, the **Gramvoússa** peninsula has to be explored on tracks – either on foot, by moped or by boat from Haniá harbour.

SOUTH COAST

The wild, unspoiled southern coast both east and west of **Hóra Sfakíon** is briefly green in winter and spring but arid the rest of the year. Two gorges, smaller than Samariá and much less popular, can be reached from Hóra Sfakíon: the **Imbrós Gorge** lies below the road as it descends to Hóra Sfakíon from the **Askífou Plateau**. The **Aradhéna Gorge** begins from the deserted village of **Aradhéna**, 4km (2½ miles) from Anópoli.

From Iráklion the road crosses the mountains and descends with panoramic views over the **Messára plain**. Following the Dorian invasion in 1100BC, **Górtyn** became an important city as the Roman capital of Cyrenaica (Crete and Libya). The famous **Law Code of Górtyn** is built into the wall of the **Roman Odeion** and the nearby **Christian Basilica of Agios Títos** (AD105) is the best-preserved in Crete.

The Minoan palace of **Phaistós** lies on a hill close to **Mirés** with superb views over the plain to the mountains beyond (open daily 08:00–20:00 in summer, and 08:00–19:00 in winter). A road runs 3km (2 miles) east along the ridge to **Agia Triádha** – once possibly a **Minoan** royal summer palace (open daily 08:00–19:00/20:00 in summer, and 08:00–15:00 in winter). The site is incomparable.

AKROTIRI

Akrotíri, the promontory to the east of Haniá, makes a worthwhile day trip. At the monastery of Agia Triádha tangerine trees surround its Venetian façade; the monastery of Moní Gouvernétou stands on a plateau 5km (3 miles) further north. A rough path leads from the latter down a rocky gorge spanned by a bridge going nowhere, and also to the monastery of Moní Katholikó which is built into the rocks.

Below: *Home of rare plants and birds, Samariá Gorge offers one of the most dramatic walks in Europe.*

Crete at a Glance

Best Times to Visit

Naturalists will want to visit in **Spring** – most flowers bloom between March and April and many villages hold Easter processions. **May–July** is best for mountain flowers but the Samaria Gorge is closed until 1 May. Beaches are crowded from **June–September** but by October they empty and the sea is still warm. **Winters** are mild and the island makes a good off-season break.

Getting There

Olympic Airways has **flights** to Crete from **Athens West terminal**: five times daily to and from **Iráklion**, three times daily to **Haniá**. There are four scheduled **flights** weekly from **Rhodes** and also three from **Thessaloníki** to **Iráklion**. In season there are many **charter flights** to both airports from UK and other European countries. **Iráklion** airport is connected with the capital by bus #1 to **Platía Eleftherías** in the centre. In **Haniá**, Olympic buses meet the company flights and many hotels have their own coaches. **Taxis** are quick and reliable. There are daily **ferry** departures from **Piraeus** to both **Iráklion** and **Haniá**. At **Haniá**, ferries dock at **Soúdha**, from where buses and taxis take you into town. You can also travel to Crete direct from the Cyclades and the Dodecanese. (see page 124 for on-line timetable and bookings).

Getting Around

Good bus services are maintained between the main Cretan towns: in **Haniá** the central bus station is on **Odhós Kidhonías**; in **Iráklion** there are four bus stations according to destinations: check departure points and times with Tourist Police.

Where to Stay

Haniá
Luxury
Amphora, 20 Parados Theotokopóulou St., tel: (0821) 93-224, fax: (0821) 93-226. Lovely 14th-century building on harbour front, nice rooms.

Mid-range
Pension Nostos, 42–46 Zambelíou, 73100, tel: (0821) 94-740. Delightful pension in back streets with 12 studios.
Doma, formerly the British Consulate, comfortable, with antiques and memorabilia.

Budget
Pension Eva, 1 Theofánous and Zambelíou St., 73100, tel: (0821) 76-706. Immaculate period-style rooms.

Iráklion
Luxury
Astoria Casis Hotel, Plateía Eleftherías, tel: (081) 343-080, fax: (081) 229-078. Central

Mid-range
Mediterranean, Smirnis St., tel: (081) 289-331, fax: (081) 289-335. Reasonable, central.

Budget
Olympic, Platía Kournárou, tel: (081) 288-861, fax: (081) 222-512. Town centre.

Réthimnon and Plakiás
Luxury
Grecotel Creta Palace, just east of Réthimnon, tel: (0831) 55-181, fax: (0831) 54-085. Hotel and bungalow complex.

Mid-range
Hotel Ideon, 10 Platía Plastíra, Réthimnon 7410, tel/fax: (0831) 28- 667. Good seafront, location, modern, pool.

Budget
Seeblick, 17 Platía Plastíra, Réthimnon 7410, tel: (0831) 22-478. Seafront location.

Hersónissos
Luxury
Aldemar Knossós Royal Village, Hersónissos 70014, tel: (0897) 23-375, fax: (0897) 23-150. Beach location, pool.

Mid-range
Maria Apartments, Hersónissos 70014, tel: (0897) 22-580. Spacious apartments.

Budget
Hotel Iro, Hersónissos 70014, tel: (0897) 22-136, fax: (0897) 23-728. Central.

Mália
Luxury
Grecotel Mália Park, Mália 70007, tel: (0897) 31-460. Bungalows in superb gardens.

Crete at a Glance

Budget
Pension Aspasia, Mália
70007, tel: (0897) 31-290.
Clean, friendly pension just
outside the old village.

Mátala
Luxury
The Valley Village, tel:
(0892) 42-776. On the
edge of village, with pool.

Mid-range
Hotel Zafira, tel: (0892)
45-112, fax: (0892) 45-725.
Reasonably priced, near town.

Budget
Coral Pension, just outside
village, tel: (0892) 42-375.

Agios Nikólaos
Luxury
Elounda Mare, tel: (0841)
41-102/3, fax: (0841) 41-307.
Superb complex of hotel
rooms, 40 bungalows.
St Nicolas Bay, tel: (0841)
25-041, fax: (0841) 24-556.
Complex with 130 bungalows.

Mid-range
Panorama, Akti Koundoúrou
St., tel: (0841) 28-890. Good
views over harbour.

WHERE TO EAT

Haniá
Dino's, Harbour. Impressive
variety of seafood dishes,
reasonably priced.
Taman, 49 Zambeliou Street.
In basement of old Turkish
bath, unusual Greek dishes
and vegetarian food.

Kings, 15 Kondiláki Street.
International cusine, seafood
and vegetarian specialities.
Konaki, 40 Kondiláki St.,
tel: (0821) 70-859. Cretan
specialites in old courtyard.

Iráklion
Gao, Platía Venizélou,
tel: (081) 243-958. Self-ser-
vice cafeteria, pasta dishes.
Giovanni, Korai St., tel: (081)
246-338. Traditional Cretan
dishes and vegetarian menu.

Rethímnon
Vangela, Platia Petiháki.
Popular, very lively and the
food is worth waiting for.

Hersoníssos
La Fontanina, Georgiou
Petraki St., tel: (0897) 22-209.
Excellent pizzeria/pasta house.
Sokaki, 10 Evagelistias St.,
tel: (0897) 23-972. Cretan
specialities at the right price.

Mália
San Georgio, on main
square, tel: (0897) 32-211.
Traditional Greek dishes.

Agios Nikólaos
Il Caprici, 31 Akti
Koundoúrou. Italian menu.

TOURS AND EXCURSIONS

Coach tours to **Knossós**,
Festos and **Agia Triádha**,
Samaria and **Vái** organized by
travel agents in main towns.
Sea cruises to Siss, Mohlos
and Psira islands (from **Agios
Nikólaos**) and Dhia (Iráklion).
Trekking and mountain
walking organized by the
Mountain Climbing Bureau,
tel: (0825) 44-946 and
tel: (0831) 55-855.

USEFUL CONTACTS

Tourist Office:
Iráklion, 1 Xanthoudídou
Street, tel: (081) 228-225.
Haniá, 18 Kriari Street,
tel: (0821) 92-943.
Réthimnon, E, Venizélou,
tel: (0831) 24-143 or 29-148.
Agios Nikólaos, 20 Akti
Koundoúrou Street, tel: (0841)
22-357, fax: (0841) 26-398.
For information in English,
tel: 131.
Tourist Police:
Iráklion, Dikeosínos Street,
tel: (081) 283-190.
Haniá, 44 Karaiskáki Street,
tel: (0821) 24-477/51-111.
Réthimnon, Plateia Heróon,
tel: (0831) 28-156.
Agios Nikólaos,
tel: (0841) 26-900.

CRETE	J	F	M	A	M	J	J	A	S	O	N	D
AVERAGE TEMP. °F	54	54	57	63	68	75	79	79	75	70	64	57
AVERAGE TEMP. °C	12	12	14	17	20	24	26	26	24	21	18	14
HOURS OF SUN DAILY	5	5	6	8	10	12	13	12	9	6	5	5
RAINFALL ins.	15	15	17	20	24	29	31	31	29	25	20	17
RAINFALL mm	5	5	6	8	10	12	13	12	9	6	5	5
DAYS OF RAINFALL	9	8	6	3	1	0	0	0	1	3	6	9

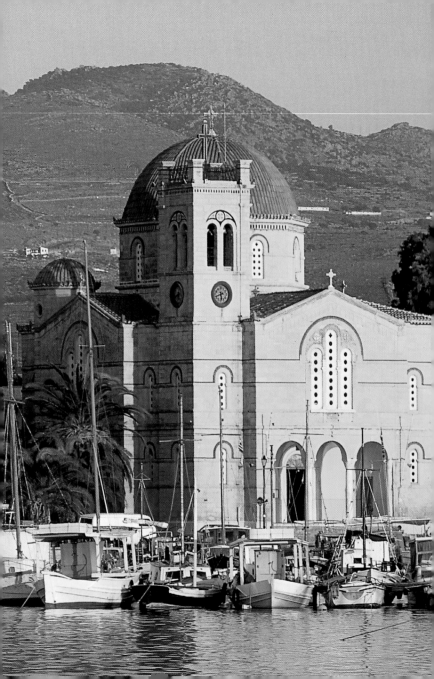

4
The Saronic Islands

Hydra (Idra), **Aegína**, **Póros**, **Salamína** (Salamis) and Spétses, the main islands of the Saronic gulf, form a rocky volcanic chain so easily reached from Athens that they virtually become suburbs in the summer. Wealthier city dwellers maintain summer homes there and the islands offer easy escape from the pace of city life and the smog. Out of season, good ferry connections are maintained and the true character of each island is revealed together with a rich array of archaeological sites.

Aegína, once a major rival to Athens, is famed for its **Temple of Aphaía** and **pistachio groves**. Nowadays many residents commute to their city workplace. Its satellite islands of **Angístri** and **Moní** offer an easy escape from the summer crowds.

The Saronic islands have been of great importance in the maritime history of Greece – **Hydra** and **Spétses** led the fleets in the War of Independence, while **Salamína** is the site of the conquest of the Persian fleet under Xerxes in 480BC. The god Poseidon has a long association with **Póros** and more recent links with literary 'demi-gods' and sages include: Henry Miller with Póros, John Fowles with Spétses and Leonard Cohen with Hydra.

For visitors to Athens there are single day **cruises** which manage to visit three islands in a day. Aegína is served by **hydrofoils** from Piraeus while those for other islands (and more leisurely services) leave from Zéa Marína. Póros lies barely 400m (1312ft) off the **Argolid Coast** of the Peloponnese and frequent boats from **Galatas** negotiate the channel.

DON'T MISS

*** Aegína: the Doric Temple of Aphaía – the best preserved temple on any of the islands.
*** Spétses: the town with pavements of black and white pebble mosaics.
** Aegína: Pérdhika with its wildlife sanctuary and fish restaurants; a great favourite with Athenians.
** Hydra: Profitis Ilias monastery and the convent of Ayios Efpráxia.
* Póros: Kalavria for the many sandy coves backed by tall pine trees.

Opposite: *The church of Ayios Nikólaos with its twin domes is a landmark at Aegina town's waterfront.*

CLIMATE

The weather of the Saronic gulf is the weather of Athens – hot and dry in summer and cold in winter – but without the smog (*néfos*). Summer visitors to Athens and residents use the Saronic islands as an escape to cleaner air.

AEGINA ★

Once a rival to Athens, Aegína (84km²; 32 sq miles) is nowadays more like one of the city's pleasanter suburbs. The first settlements date from 3000BC and the island was the first (650BC) to mint coinage in Europe. Its coins, imprinted with a turtle, have turned up all around the Mediterranean. In 1828 it became the first capital of free Greece and appropriately minted the first *drachma*.

Behind the façade of shops selling pottery and pistachios, Aegína town maintains a certain elegance through its neo-Classical 19th-century architecture. The curved waterfront with its fishing boats and chapel of **Agios Nikólaos** is a popular place for an evening stroll (*volta*) and for spectacular sunsets. **Kolóna**, where the ancient city stood, overlooks the 'secret' port (only locals knew how to reach it): a single column marks the site of a 5th-century **Temple of Apollo**.

In the centre of the island is the monastery of **Agios Nektaríos**, a popular place with pilgrims. Above it lies the ruined and deserted Byzantine town of **Paleochóra** which was attacked twice by pirates; in 1538 and 1654. Approximately 20 of Paleochóra's 365 churches still stand – those with frescoes include the **Cathedral of the Episkopí**, **Chapel of Taxiárchis** and **Basilica of Agios Anárgyroi**; a **Venetian castle** looms over the

Below: *The Temple of Aphaía on Aegína is the best preserved of all island temples.*

old town. The superb Doric **Temple of Aphaía** stands on a pine covered hill high above **Mesagrós**.

Twenty five of a total of 32 columns still stand, making it the finest temple on any island. Parian marble was used for the magnificent pediment sculptures depicting the **Trojan War**, which now languish in Munich after being saved in 1812 from peasants who smashed marble for their limekilns. Aphaía was the local name for a goddess worshipped almost exclusively on Aegína: later she was identified with Artemis. Many finds from the temple are now in the **Archaeological Museum** in Aegína town.

The island's third temple – the **Temple of Hellanion Zeus** – lies on the slopes of **Mt Oros** (534m; 1706ft) where only a monumental staircase and two terraces are visible but the top of the mountain is worth the one hour's walk for the superb views over the Saronic Gulf.

There are very pleasant beaches south of Aegína at **Aiginitíssa**, **Marathónas** and **Pérdhika**. The unique wildlife sanctuary in Pérdhika takes in wounded and sick creatures from all over Greece and carries out a programme reintroducing them into the wild. One success is the population of **kri-kri** – Cretan wild goats (*see* pp. 10 and 42) established on **Moní** out in the bay.

ANGÍSTRI **

Most of the 700 inhabitants of Angístri (hook island) are of Albanian descent. Tourism is concentrated at **Skála** which has the best beach, leaving the rest of the fertile, wooded island remarkably peaceful and unspoiled. The island is only 17km² (7 sq miles) in area.

AEGINA PEANUTS

Aegína is the main producer of pistachios – locally known as 'Aegína Peanuts'. Canvas sheets are spread beneath the trees in late August and the nuts knocked on to them. After hulling, the nuts are soaked in sea water and dried on flat roofs and terraces in the sun. Local abundance is not reflected in the prices charged in town.

Hydra (Idra) *

The barren, 52km² (20 sq miles) island of Hydra was settled by **Greek** and **Albanian** refugees from Epirus in the 15th century. The newcomers became sailors and flourished under **Ottoman** rule through trade and piracy.

The waterfront is spectacular as you appproach its ranked rows of restored grey and white Italianate mansions (*archontíka*) by ferry. No cars are allowed on the island and many of its affluent visitors stray no further than the chic boutiques and hair-dressing salons. Crowds are quickly left behind as you walk inland to the convent of **Agia Efpráxia** and **Profítis Ilías Monastery**

Above: *Elegant stone mansions overlook the harbour on Hydra. Once the homes of sea captains, they have been taken over by artists and other creative folk.*

Below: *Fresh vegetables on sale on the harbour at Pérdhika, a pretty resort surrounded by abundant pistachio groves.*

– taxi donkeys are available – or along the coast to **Vlíchos** and to **Kastéllo** with its fort, or to **Limióniza Bay** on the southern side of the island. The infamous cliffs at **Mólos** are said to have been the point of forced departure of the aged, incapable of working for their living. Caiques take about an hour to reach **Dokós**, an islet of hard marble (*marmarópita*) known to divers as the site of a 3000-year-old wreck discovered by Jacques Cousteau.

Póros **

With a population of approximately 4500 and a total area of 28km² (11 sq miles), two islands, **Kalávria** and **Sferiá** make up Póros. It is the darling of UK package

tours and cruise and ferry ships which ply the narrow straits of Póros (370m; 1214ft wide) – everyone is guaranteed to be on deck for the experience.

The wooded beaches of the north are popular with holiday-makers while away from the sea the two main foci of interest are the peaceful monastery of **Zoodóchos Pigí** in the southeast of the island

and the **Temple of Poseidon**
in the northeast – an impov-
erished ruin summed up in
the local name 'five stones'.
Regular ferries make it easy
to include mainland trips to
the Peloponnese while
based here and the list
of possibilities reads like
a catalogue of ancient
Greek history: **Epidaúros**,
Nafplíon, **Mycenae**…

SALAMÍNA (SALAMIS) *

The ferry to **Paloukía**, the main island's port, takes a few
minutes from **Pérama**, west of Piraeus. In many respects
the island (area 93.5km^2; 36 sq miles) is a suburb of
Athens, allowing an escape from the smog, if not the
local pollution which makes swimming on Salamína a
risk. Pine-covered Mt Profitis Ilías near Salamína town
(**Kouloúri**) offers good views over the mainland, and
the **Convent of Faneroméni**, built from a much earlier
temple, is a popular picnic spot. Regular bus services
make it possible to reach the south of the island and the
abandoned monastery of **Agios Nikólaos**.

SPÉTSES ***

Many visitors are drawn to Spétses (area 22.5km^2; 9 sq
miles), furthest of the Saronic islands from Athens,
through the spell woven by John Fowles in his novel *The
Magus*, set on Spétses. The whole harbour area in the
capital is named after a distinctive square (Dápia) paved
with black and white pebbles leading to the water. Just off
the square is **Anárgyros** and **Korgialénios College**, now
closed. The town **Museum** is housed in the 18th-century
mansion of Hadziyiánnis Mexís (open Tuesday–Sunday
08:00–14:00). The attractive old harbour, **Paléo Limáni**, is
a place for yachts, fishermen and caique builders – the
nearby cathedral of **Agios Nikólaos** was where the flag of
Independence was raised in 1821.

Above: *Spétses is
justifiably popular with
families for its safe beaches
of pebbles and shingle.*

LASKARINA BOUBOULINA

On 2 April 1821, Spétses
became the first Greek
island to raise the flag of
Independence. The island's
fleet figured large in battles
against the Ottomans under
the command of **Laskarina
Bouboulina**, the island's lady
admiral and mother of six
who, if the battle looked
more bloody on shore, would
abandon ship and set off
with her sabre.
  She was a skilled tactician
and inspirational leader who
could outdo any man in
the drinking stakes, so it is
perhaps to preserve fragile
male egos that she is reputed
to have been extremely ugly.

54

The Saronic Islands at a Glance

BEST TIMES TO VISIT

Spring, from March–April, brings green to the islands and a profusion of flowers. Throughout the year the islands are a haven for Athenians escaping at weekends – especially in **summer** when the smog in the city is at its worst. **Winters** are mild and foreign visitors on the islands few and far between.

GETTING THERE

Passenger **ferries** and tourist **boats** for all Saronic ports (including Angístri) leave from Piraeus central harbour daily (also **car ferries** for Aegína and Póros). Only **hydrofoils** for Aegína leave from the main port of **Piraeus**; hydrofoils for other Saronic ports (including Aegína at certain times) leave from **Zéa Marína**. **Aegína** – hourly **hydrofoil** or **ferry** until dusk from **Piraeus**, often connections with Saronic islands and Méthana. **Port Authority**, tel: (0297) 22-328. **Hydra** - daily **ferry** connections to other Saronic islands. Frequent **hydrofoil** connections to Póros, Spétses and mainland (Pórto Chéli, Ermióni, Náfplion), less often to Kíthera and Monemvásia. **Port Authority**, tel: (0298) 52-279. **Póros** – car ferries from Piraeus, Aegína and Méthana daily: every half hour to Galatás on the mainland. Frequent hydrofoils daily. **Port Authority**, tel: (0298) 22-274. **Salamína** – ferry from Pérama

to Paloukía every 15 min and 5 per day from Piraeus. **Port Authority Athens**, tel: (01) 465-3252.**Spétses** – ferries and hydrofoils daily from Piraeus and other Saronic islands. Sometimes from Kýthera and Peloponnese ports (including Kósta). **Port Authority**, tel: (0298) 72-245.

GETTING AROUND

On **Aegína** a good bus service runs from town (Platía Ethneyersias) to most villages and sites; caiques link Aegína town with **Angístri** and **Pérdika** with **Moní**. On **Hydra** water taxis operate from the quay to beaches and the islet of **Dokós**. On **Póros** one bus only to the monastery and back. **Salamína** has a bus service operating between villages. **Spétses** relies on horse-drawn carriages, scooters and bicycles. (see page 124 for on-line timetables and bookings).

WHERE TO STAY

Aegína town
LUXURY
Aeginotiko Archhontiko, tel: (0297) 24-968, fax: (0297) 26-716. An up-market pension.

MID-RANGE
Nausica, tel: (0297) 22-333, fax: (0297) 22-477. Bungalow complex, in pleasant gardens.

BUDGET
Danae, tel: (0297) 22-424, fax: (0297) 26-509. A modest-sized hotel, right on the beach.

Souvála
MID-RANGE
Galaxy, tel/fax: (0297) 52-944. Small pension, family run. **Xanthippi**, tel (0297) 52-201. Furnished apartments, clean.

Agia Marína
MID-RANGE
Apollo, tel: (0297) 32-271, fax: (0297) 32-688. Sea front, quiet with swimming pool. **Blue Fountain**, tel: (0297) 32-644, fax: (0297) 32-052. Comfortable, friendly. **Piccadilly**, tel: (0297) 32-696, fax: (0297) 32-206. Sea views from most rooms.

Perdika
LUXURY
Moondy Bay Bungalows Profitis Ilías, tel: (0297) 61-622, fax: (0297) 61-147. Rooms air conditioned, sports facilities. **Aegína Maris**, tel: (0297) 25-130. Hotel bungalow complex in landscaped garden.

Angístri
MID-RANGE
Spastiras, tel: (0297) 91-218. Furnished apartments – clean and comfortable.

Hydra
LUXURY
Bratsera, Tombazi St., tel: (0298) 53-970, fax: (0298) 52-53-626. Air conditioning and pool; closed November. **Miramare**, tel: (0298) 52-300, fax: (0298) 52-301. Pension; boat link to harbour, water sports; open April–October.

The Saronic Islands at a Glance

Orloff, tel: (0298) 52-564, fax: (0298) 53-532. In superbly restored mansion.

MID-RANGE

Amaryllis, tel: (0298) 52-249, fax: (0298) 53-611. An old mansion, very comfortable.

Póros

LUXURY

Sirena, close to monastery, tel: (0298) 22-741, fax: (0298) 22-744. Private beach, casino. Open April–October.

Neon Aegli, Askéli beach, tel: (0298) 22-372, fax: (0298) 24-345. Every room with balcony. Private beach, watersports.

MID-RANGE

Possidonion, tel: (0298) 22-770. Small set of comfortably furnished apartments.

Villa Tryfon, tel: (0298) 25-854, fax: (0298) 22-215. All rooms with kitchen facilities; views of port and town.

Salamína

MID-RANGE

Gabriel Hotel, in Eantion, tel: (01) 466-2223, fax: (01) 466-2275. The best on the island; open April–September.

Akroyiali, Themistokléous St., tel: (01) 467-3363. Comfortable pensions.

Spétses

LUXURY

Possidonion tel: (0298) 72-308, fax: (0298) 72-208. Renovated but still the place to stay; open April–October.

Villa Jasemia, tel: (0298) 72-314, fax: (0298) 72-872. Pricey but heaven for the ardent John Fowles admirer.

Akroyiali, Agia Anárgyri, tel: (0298) 73-695, fax: (0298) 74-054. Pension on the best beach.

BUDGET

Villa Christina, tel: (0298) 72-218. Good central location, very comfortable pension.

Faros, tel: (0928) 72-613, fax: (0928) 72-614. Basic, friendly.

WHERE TO EAT

Aegína

Agorá, right next to the fish market. Serves sea-fresh fish.

Nodos, Perdika. Presents seafood of a high standard.

Vatsoulia's, near Temple of Aphaia. Very popular with the locals (open on weekends and Wednesdays only).

Hydra

Christina's Palace, Kamini Beach. Traditional Greek cooking, attractively priced.

Douskos, near the Cathedral. Greek food served in a cool and pleasant courtyard.

The Three Brothers, near the Cathedral. Popular with taverna food superbly cooked.

Spétses

Patralis, to the right of the harbour. Fresh fish beautifully cooked and worth the price.

Stelios, near Klimis Hotel. Wide range of vegetarian and fish dishes.

Taverna Tassos, Agios Anárgyri. Hard to beat Greek food at realistic prices.

Salamína. Patronized mainly by Greeks, inexpensive food.

Kasnellos, Kakei Vígla. The restaurant is lauded for its fish.

Vassilis, Selínia. Also serves excellent fish dishes.

TOURS AND EXCURSIONS

Good connections with other Saronic islands and with the mainland make day trips easy: from **Póros** it is simple to explore the **Peloponnese**. Organized trips are advertised by town travel agents.

USEFUL CONTACTS

Tourist Police:

Aegína, Vass. Georgíou Street, tel: (0297) 22-100.

Hydra, Odhós Votsi Street, tel: (0298) 52-205.

Póros, on harbour, tel: (0298) 22-462.

Spétses, Botassi Street, tel: (0298) 73-100.

SARONIC ISLANDS	J	F	M	A	M	J	J	A	S	O	N	D
AVERAGE TEMP. °F	46	46	52	59	68	75	82	81	75	68	57	50
AVERAGE TEMP. °C	8	8	11	15	20	24	28	27	24	20	14	10
HOURS OF SUN DAILY	5	5	6	7	10	11	12	11	9	7	5	4
RAINFALL ins.	2	2	2	2	1	0.5	0.5	0.5	0.5	2.5	3	2
RAINFALL mm	59	48	50	43	22	12	10	14	14	65	77	55
DAYS OF RAINFALL	11	10	10	9	7	4	2	3	3	8	10	12

5
The Cyclades

The 56 islands of the 'Kyklades', 24 of which are inhabited, form a loose ring (*kyklos* = circle), roughly centred on the sacred island of **Délos**. Apart from **Andros** (an extension of nearby **Evia**), volcanic **Thíra** (Santoríni), **Kéa**, **Náxos** and **Sérifos**, the islands share a common legacy of rocky landscapes with no forests.

Dazzling white 'cubic' houses crowd hillsides forming the town or **Chóra** and small, enclosed harbours finger a sea of unbelievable crystal clarity. This is the island Greece of picture postcards – tiny chapels, windmills, donkeys and narrow labyrinthine alleyways. Their appeal dates back to 3000BC when the first civilization was established there.

The Cyclades are the island hopper's favourite: **Mýkonos** is a magnet for hedonists with superb beaches and the best nightlife, followed by **Ios** which has great charm. **Náxos** and **Páros** are extremely busy with package tours in August but, away from the resort towns, they have escaped mass development. **Folégandros**, **Mílos** and **Amorgós** are for those who want quiet while **Koufoníssi**, **Skinoússa** and **Heráklia** near Náxos are for those who wish to escape altogether. **Tínos** has long been a spiritual centre in the Orthodox church and a favourite with Greeks; **Sýros**, the administrative capital, has an elegant town. **Délos**, a religious and commercial centre in Classical times, is an archaeologist's paradise, easily reached by caique from **Mýkonos**. Volcanic **Thíra** with the improbable contrasts of dark rocks, deep azure sea and white houses is a great favourite with travellers.

DON'T MISS

*** **Mýkonos:** the white-washed town (Chóra) and delightful 'little Venice'.
*** **Sífnos:** and its ornate Venetian dovecotes.
*** **Thíra (Santoríni):** its volcanic scenery and Akrotíri with its buried Minoan town.
** **Kéa:** Ioulís with red pan-tiled houses and its windmills.
* **Délos:** island sanctuary of Apollo known for the Delian Lions and many other remarkable antiquities.

Opposite: *The clean lines of Cycladic architecture are typified by Dhía on Thíra, with dazzling white buildings and blue domes set against black volcanic rocks.*

Above: *Chozoviótissa monastery on Amorgos set against a steep cliff face.*
Opposite: *Batsí, the main tourist centre on Andros.*

THE BACK ISLANDS

Between Amorgós and Náxos lies a chain of six small islands with idyllic beaches and superb walks. Most accommodation is with island families and it helps to have some basic Greek.
• **Donoússa:** difficult to reach but lovely beaches and walks.
• **Iráklia:** popular with day-trippers, has an old Chóra and a cave with impressive stalactites and stalagmites.
• **Keros:** once a centre of Cycladic culture.
• **Koufoníssi:** claims to be the smallest inhabited island pair (3.8km²; 1½ sq miles) in Greece – long beaches at Finikas and Pori.
• **Skinoússa:** completely unspoilt with nine low hills and three windmills.

AMORGÓS *

The thick oak woods of Amorgós were destroyed by fire in the 19th century leaving its rugged mountains bare. It is still a wild, unspoiled and, above all friendly island (area 134km²; 52 sq miles), even though its popularity with tourists increases year by year.

Katápola, the main port, is watched over by a string of derelict windmills and lies tucked into a bay below the main town of **Chóra**. The walls of Chóra's **Venetian Castle** (built 1290) enclose 40 chapels and one of them, **Agios Fanoúrios**, is claimed to be the smallest chapel in Greece.

A walk uphill from Chóra brings you to **Minoa**, famous in antiquity and once one of the island's three important towns where there are remains of a gymnasium, acropolis and **Temple to Apollo**. A rubble path (*kalderími*) from Chóra drops towards **Chozoviótissa Monastery** – an astonishing place, whose whitewashed bulk seems to be plastered to the cliff face (open daily 08:00–14:00 and 17:00–20:00).

Órmos Aigialis, the second 'port', has a good sandy bay and seven old windmills. Buses connect twice a day with **Katápola** but Egiáli is more easily reached by boat and more spectacularly accessed on foot along the ridge with views out to **Nikoúria**, a fomer leper colony.

ANÁFI **

Tourism is in an embryonic stage in **Anáfi**, southernmost of the Cyclades. The friendly island with lovely beaches is a place for those who crave peace and isolation – boats can be withdrawn if sea conditions deteriorate. **Chóra**, the island's one village, is a short but steep walk from the jetty at **Agios Nikólaos**. A path leads east of Chóra via deserted **Katalimátsa** to the **Monastery of Panayía Kalamiótissa** perched on the eastern peninsula.

ANDROS *

Mainland Greeks have been the main tourist visitors to Andros and the island has its quota of resident mega-wealthy Athenian shipping families. The mountainous landscape offers great contrasts between a well-forested south and a parched north. Total land area is approximately 380km² (147 sq miles).

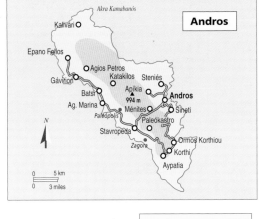

Gávrion is the main port but hydrofoils and taxi boats to coves along the south use **Batsí**, the main tourist centre. The ruins of **Paleópolis**, the ancient capital, lie on a steep hill and are reached by a flight of over 1000 steps from the modern village of the same name. A spectacularly terraced valley connects **Batsí** to **Andros (Chóra)**, the windy capital with neo-Classical mansions belonging to ship owners.

Andros town has several attractive churches (Agios Thalassíni, Agios Geórgios) and two excellent museums endowed by the Goulandrís family: the **Archaeology Museum** which is famous for the Hermes of Ándros (open Tuesday–Sunday 08:30–15:00) and the **Museum of Modern Art** which features works by Bouzianis, Manolidis and Tómbros (open Wednesday–Monday 10:00–14:00 and 18:00–21:00).

Inland the villages are decked with flowers in spring and offer plenty of walks to: **Apíkia** (famed for its mineral water), **Steniés** (regarded as the prettiest village on Andros) and **Ménites** with springs and the church of **Panayias tis Koumoúlous**.

A PORT IN A STORM

According to Greek legend,
Anáfi was created by Apollo
for Jason and the Argonauts
in need of a no-frills (and no
water) berth during a storm.
A **Temple to Apollo** later
stood on the island, built by a
grateful Jason, but its stone
was apparently used to build
a monastery – Zoodóchos Pigí.

TOURIST INFORMATION

Amorgós, tel: (0285) 71-257.
Íos, tel: (0286) 91-505/91-222.
Mílos, tel: (0287) 21-370.
Mýkonos, tel: (0289) 22-482.
Náxos, tel: (0285) 22-717.
Páros, tel: (0284) 21-222.
Sífnos, tel: (0284) 31-10.

ANTÍPAROS *

A narrow channel now separates Páros from **Antíparos** –
whereas in antiquity they were united by a causeway.
Apart from good beaches at **Kástro**, **Agios Georgios** and
Sifnaíkos Yialós, the island's main attraction is a cave
which has been drawing tourists since the time of
Alexander the Great. The cave is reached by boat from
Kástro (also **Paroíkia** and **Poúnda** in summer) and then
a half-hour walk or donkey ride. The main chamber is
70m (230ft) below ground – names of former visitors
carved on the walls include the poet Byron.

Off the coast lie several islets: **Strogilónisi** and
Despotikó are hunting reserves and **Sáliagos** is the site
of a Neolithic fishing village.

DÉLOS ***

You can only visit Délos (usually from Mýkonos) on a day
trip, unless you have a permit to stay. The island was the
most important classical shrine to **Apollo**, as birthplace of
the god and **Artemis**, his twin. The antiquities are
revealed as you step off the boat – to the left of the landing

stage is the **Agora of the Competalists**.
Délos was an important trade centre
and here the ancients left offerings to
the **Lares Competales**: minor Roman
gods who were patrons of trades.

The bare road to the **Sanctuary of
Apollo** was once lined with statues –
there were three temples built to the
god, the largest built in 476BC by the
Delians themselves. The **Terrace of
the Lions** with its five stylized beasts
is the outstanding feature of the religious part of the site. A theatre with a
capacity for 5500 stands in the area
south of the jetty and next to it an
impressive arched reservoir. Nearby
villas give a vivid indication of life for
the privileged with superb mosaics
from the Hellenistic and Roman ages.

FOLÉGANDROS *

Sheer cliffs rising from the sea give Folégandros (total area 32km²; 12 sq miles) its palpable air of wildness: hundreds of 'dissidents' were exiled here during the Junta. **Chóra**, the capital, is a delightful town perched 300m (984ft) above the sea and reached by a new road from the harbour.

The **Kástro**, the Venetian fortress built by Marco Sanudo (13th century), is a maze of alleyways and balconied houses where craft shops cater for a more discerning clientèle. From nearby **Análypsi** there are views down both coasts and a short walk brings you to the '**golden cave**' (*Chrísispiliá*) with its stalactites and stalagmites.

Above: *The stylized Lions of Délos have 'guarded' the shrine to Apollo for more than 2000 years.*
Opposite: *Windmills like this one in Antíparos are a familiar site near ports.*

IOS **

The reputation of Ios as a mecca to a free-living (but too poor to be free-spending) young began in the 1960s. It is still the place where being older than 30 is to be geriatric.

Although campsites have been provided, 'tradition' suggests that the beach is the place to party the night away and sleep. However, police are becoming less tolerant of this because of theft and several deaths (alcohol poisoning). Water is very scarce – a flushing loo is a luxury in high summer.

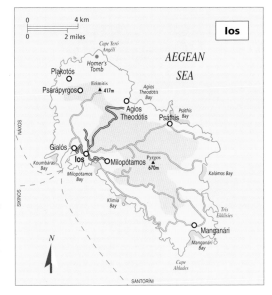

0   4 km
0   2 miles

Ios

Cape Yeró
Angéli

AEGEAN SEA

Plakotós
Homer's Tomb
Erimitis
Psárápyrgos
▲ 417m
Agios Theodótis Bay
Agios Theodótis
Psáthis
Psáthis Bay
NAXOS
Gialós
Koumbáras Bay
Ios
Milopótamos
Pyrgos ▲ 670m
Milopótamos Bay
Kalámos Bay
SIKINOS
Klimía Bay
Tris Ekklísies
N
Manganári
Manganári Bay
Cape Ahládes
SANTORINI

Above: *Crystal clear seas and guaranteed sunshine make Ios a tourist idyll.*

Visitors throng to the beaches – within easy reach of the port of **Gialós** – one of which, **Milopótamos** (Milopótas), claims to be among the best in the Cyclades and is served by buses from Ios town. Another resort, **Koumbáras**, has a pretty, sandy cave. Ios town has great charm behind the façade developed to cater for tourists – visitors can find a dozen windmills, ancient olive presses and ancient walls.

KÉA (TZIA) ★★

Set apart from the rest of the group, **Kéa** (area 131km²; 51 sq miles) is popular with foreigners keen on walking in its landscape of terraced hills and lush valleys peppered with red pantiled houses, windmills and tiny churches.

In Classical times responsible citizens of Kéa were expected to drink a brimming cup of hemlock on reaching their allotted three score and ten years.

Korissía, the port, is set in **Agios Nikólaos** bay, a deep natural harbour about 6km (4 miles) from the main town of Ioulís (**Chóra**) which sits between two hillsides. The town's **Venetian fortress** (1210) occupies the site of ancient Ioulís from which there are superb views over the north of the island. To the northeast of the town is the sphinx-like **Lion of Kéa** carved in the 6th century BC from a rocky outcrop. Good beaches are to be found at **Písses**, **Vourkári**, **Otzías** and **Koundoúros**.

KÍMOLOS ★

Although the northern half of the island is dusty and scarred by open-cast mining (cimolite), the south is delightfully unspoiled (total area 38km²; 15 sq miles). **Psáthi**, the port, is set below the capital (**Chóra**) which comprises two settlements: **Exo Kástro** outside the castle walls has a few tavernas and also the **Church of Panayia Evangelístra** (1614); **Mésa Kástro**, a maze of small alley ways and old houses, lies within the walls.

VENUS DE MILO

In 1820, a farmer planting corn on Milos discovered a cave containing half a statue of an amply proportioned Aphrodite. A French officer encouraged him to look for the rest of the statue – he found it together with 6th-century statues of Hermes and Hercules, probably a hoard hidden from early Christians bent on destroying pagan images. It now resides in the Louvre – the officer's drawing showed pedestal and arms.

KÝTHNOS **

Barren and mountainous **Kýthnos** (area 86km²; 33 sq miles) is an unspoiled island with innumerable small bays around its jagged coastline. Iron ore was mined on the island until 1940. **Messária (Chóra)**, the capital, is an attractive, typically Cycladic town with the pretty churches of **Agios Sávvas** and **Agia Triádha** and several of its traditional houses open for view.

It is possible to walk from Chóra down to **Agios Stefános** beach or along the ridge to **Dryópida**, once the capital and famed for its ceramics; the upper village (**Galátas**) is a wonderful labyrinth of paved lanes with a single pottery workshop.

The mildly radioactive thermal spring of **Loutrá** is popular with elderly Greeks convinced of its efficacy. The oldest known habitation in the Cyclades (7500–6000BC) has been found near Loutrá.

MÍLOS *

Mining has long been the economic mainstay of Mílos – **obsidian** (volcanic glass) was first mined and traded in Neolithic times. Nowadays **China clay** (kaolin) is mined and exported – a legacy of the volcanic heritage which has left Mílos with hot springs bubbling up from underground and a large variety of mineral deposits.

Adámas, the port, is in a sunken caldera, now the sandy bay of Mílos. **Pláka**, the capital, is a whitewashed chóra gloriously viewed as the sun sets from the chapels (**Panayia Skiniótissa** and **Panayia Thalassítras**) on the volcanic hill above. The busy,surrounding villages of **Plákes**, **Péra Triovássalos** and **Tripití** house the bulk of the island's population. Pláka's **Archaeological Museum** has some superb ceramics from **Philakópi** (open Tuesday–Sunday 08:30– 15:00). The old cobbled road – *kaldiméri* – leads to **Klíma**, a marvellously photogenic fishing village with brightly coloured boat houses. The total area of the island covers about 161km² (62 sq miles).

A GEOLOGICAL TOUR

Volcanic Milós has a number of spectacular archeological oddities. Near **Demenayáki** are disused obsidian mines and at **Mávra Gremma** are black rocks with tortured shapes. Here too, the sea bubbles furiously as a result of hot springs on the seabed. Excursions run from **Adámas** to the honeycombed, basalt islets of **Glaroníssia** with their curious groups of rock pillars.

In the southeastern village of **Sikia** a cave is dramatically illuminated by shafts of light while a little distance east is **Kleftíko**, a pirate lair which has cream and white rocks.

The bright blue pool at **Papafrángas** is ringed by rocks while at **Paleoréma** water is emerald green.

Below: *Campaniles (bell towers) are a feature of many island churches.*

Above: *Picturesque old houses stand on the seafront in Mýkonos town.*

MÝKONOS ★★★

Mýkonos (area 88km²; 34 sq miles) may be barren and windy but its superb beaches and the non-stop party atmosphere in its cosmopolitan town make it a powerful magnet for hedonists.

Mýkonos town (**Chóra**) has attractions other than bars, restaurants and clubs: the **Archaeological Museum** has finds from Rhinía (the cemetery island for Délos). Open Tuesday–Sunday 08:30–15:00. Much-photographed windmills overlook the harbour and one is a windmill museum. A row of tall, galleried Venetian houses – **Little Venice** – has survived by the sea.

Beaches abound: near the town, **Platís Gialós** is the main family beach (trips to Délos leave from here); **Paradise** and **Super Paradise** (once a mainly gay beach, now mixed) are for those after the all-over tan – there is a good daily bus service connecting resorts with Mýkonos. **Dragonísi** islet off the west coast has numerous sea caves where monk seals used to breed.

ON THE BEACH

Visitors to **Náxos** are spoilt for choice when it comes to beaches: busiest are **Agia Anna**, **Agios Prokópios** and **Pláka** offering a wide range of watersports. **Kastráki**, with white sands and crystal seas, is less busy and very safe for children. This coast is sheltered from the *meltémi* but reed-filled marshes behind the beaches can make mosquitoes a nuisance.

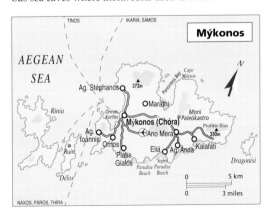

NÁXOS ★★★

Náxos, the largest of the Cyclades islands (448km²; 173 sq miles) has fertile soils supporting citrus and potatoes, silver sand beaches on its west coast and an interior with high brooding mountains.

Náxos (**Chóra**), the main port and town, is a Cycladic maze of narrow, twisting streets. The lower town – **Boúrgos** where the Greeks lived – has a beautiful Orthodox cathedral (**Metropolis of Zoodóchos Pigí**) built from remains of the earlier churches. In **Kástro**, the upper part, 19 houses still bear their coats-of-arms;

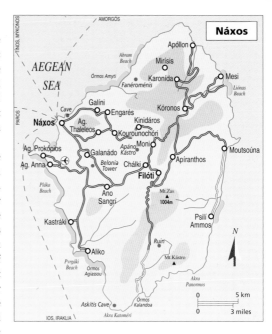

the old walls and Marco Sanudo's palace have almost disappeared but his 13th-century Catholic cathedral remains. Náxos has a lively waterfront and promenade replete with cafés: in August there is the **Dionysia** – a festival of music, dance, food and wine is held in the main square. Dionysos apparently taught the Naxians how to make wine.

On the slopes of **Mt Zas** (1004m; 3294ft) at the head of the lovely **Tragéa Valley**, lies **Filóti** with two attractive churches built mainly from marble. Good walks lead from here to the summit of Mt Zas or to the Hellenistic tower of **Chimárou**, built by the Greek, Ptolemy.

Below: *A huge, stone figure (*Kouros*) of Apollo lies near the entrance to a marble quarry close to the lovely village of Apóllon.*

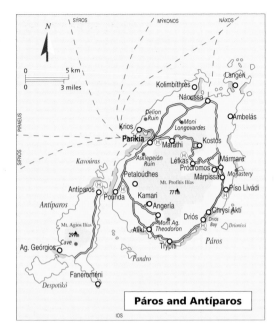

Páros and Antíparos

PÁROS ★★

In ancient Greece Páros was famed for its marble, still found at important sites everywhere except on Páros, where little of archaeological importance survives. **Mólos** and **Driós** are great beaches and **Chrysí Aktí** is superb and a paradise for windsurfers. Páros now rivals Ios for the abundance and energy of its nightlife. Out of season the fertile island is delightful and **Parikía** in particular recaptures Cycladic charm with its windmill, narrow streets filled with white houses and blue-domed buildings.

West of the town lies the Church of a Hundred Doors (**Ekatontapylianí**): Emperor Justinian ordered building to commence in the 6th century but earthquakes have forced rebuilding several times since. The town's **Archaeology Museum** has a section of the 'Parian Chronicles' – an ancient history of Greece (open Tuesday–Saturday 08:30–15:00). The rest of these marble tablets are in the Ashmolean Museum in Oxford, Britain.

The famed Parian marble was quarried at **Maráthi**, east of **Parikía** – last worked for marble for Napoleon's tomb. Márpissa, a very pretty village, has a ruined Venetian fortress, windmills and the monastery of **Agios Antónios** – beautifully built in marble and containing exceptional wall paintings. **Náoussa** is a fishing village and favourite of jet-setters – there is a half-submerged Venetian fort near the harbour.

Páros, like Rhodes, boasts a 'butterfly valley' – **Petaloúdhes** – at Psychopiáni south of Parikiá where Jersey tiger moths collect in summer before mating.

SÉRIFOS ★★★

Numerous remote sandy bays dotted around a dramatic rocky coast make Sérifos an island gem (194km²; 75 sq miles). Most visitors are housed in and around the port of **Livádi** where many of the stone houses have been bought and tastefully restored. Livadi has a good beach and two others nearby – **Livadákia** and **Karávi**. More remote beaches accessible by foot or motorcycle are **Agios Sostís**, **Chalára**, **Yialós**, **Gianéma**, **Lia**, **Platys** and **Psíli Ammos** .

SÍFNOS ★★

The terraced hills of Sífnos are laced with villages and its landscape dotted with tiny chapels, classical towers and Venetian dovecotes.

Apollonia, the sleepy capital, is visible from afar as a circle of white. Its name comes from an old **Temple of Apollo**, buried beneath the 18th-century **Church of Panayia Ouranofóra**. The island's claim to fame is its pottery – the **Museum of Popular Arts and Folklore** has a collection together with traditonal embroidery and costume (open daily 10:00–13:00 and 18:00–22:00). The best beach is at **Vathi** along the south coast, reached by caique from **Kamáres** or along a track from **Platis Gialos**.

SÍKINOS ★★

On unspoiled Síkinos transport is on foot or by donkey and there are superb walks over terraced hills with their olives and vines. The name Oenoe (**wine island**) was once used in reference to Síkinos.

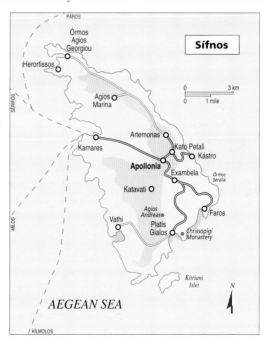

Above: *Dark volcanic cliffs contrast dramatically with shining white Firá, capital of the island of Thíra (Santoríni).*

Kástro, a double village linking two hills, is a delightful whitewashed settlement perched high above the sea. The main square is formed by balconied houses and its environs are threaded by narrow alleys with tiny shops and cafés.

SÝROS ★★

The graceful neo-Classical buildings of **Ermopoúlis** have much-faded charm – the **Catholic Quarter** is a labyrinth of small streets with several remarkable churches: the Catholic Cathedral of **St George**, **Agios Nikólaos** and **Capuchin Convent of St Jean**.

Plateía Miaoúlis, north of the harbour, is dominated by the town hall; behind the square is the **Apóllon Theatre,** a copy of La Scala in Milan. Nearby is the **Velissarópoulos Mansion** with its elaborate wall and ceiling paintings. The grand mansions of the **Vaporía Quarter** form an 'amphitheatre' above the sea with marble steps leading to the town's beaches.

The north offers small secluded beaches and ancient sites: north of the village of Halandrianí is **Kástri**, the largest early Cycladic village yet discovered.

THÍRA (SANTORINI) ★★★

The fascination of this dark, 88km^2 (34 sq miles) volcanic rock pile tightens its grip as you approach its striated cliffs – the rim of a sunken volcano. Every suitable square metre is cultivated with tiny sweet tomatoes, pistachios and grapes. The island's wines are some of Greece's best and mostly made from Assyrtíko grapes.

The whitewashed capital of **Firá** teeters high on the rim of the caldera nearly 600 stone steps above **Skála Firá** where most boats to the island berth. At close quarters tourist development shatters any romantic illusions about Firá. But away from the capital the island is fascinating. The **Archaeological Museum** houses many treasures found in Akrotíri and Mésa Voúna plus Cycladic figures.

A VOLCANIC TOWN

The first inhabitants of **Thíra** (from **Karia**) were ousted by the Minoans whose extensive colony at **Akrotíri** was destroyed by a volcanic eruption in 1450BC. In 1967 the archaeologist Marinátos began to dig at Akrotiri where **Minoan** vases had been found. The discovery of a complete Minoan colony buried in volcanic *tephra* complete with marvellous frescoes and ceramics was the find of the century.

A dramatic path along the rim of the caldera leads to **Firostefáni** and **Imerovígli**, well known for traditional barrel-roofed cave houses (skaftá). **Oía**, once a major fishing port, was damaged in an earthquake in 1956. It is a marvellous place to watch the sunset.

Black sands which become searingly hot in the sun feature at crowded **Kamarí** and **Périssa** (the best beach). Between the two lies **Ancient Thíra**, famous for its mosaics, theatre and terraced houses. Inland the **Monastery of Profítis Ilías** sits atop the island's highest point from where, on a clear day, Crete is visible.

> **THE GOLDEN ICON**
>
> An icon believed to have been painted by St Luke was discovered on Tínos in 1822. Following a vision Sister Pelagia, a nun at Kechrovouni Convent, was directed to the location of the icon beneath a rock. The icon, known as the **Megalochori** (Great Grace), is now encased in gold and reputed to have great healing powers.

TÍNOS **

The island of Tínos is sometimes billed as the 'Lourdes of the Aegean' thanks to the supposed healing powers of an icon in the **Church of Panayía Evangelístra**. The closest beach to town is Áyia Fokás – both **Xerés** and **Pórto** further east are better but busy. **Kiónia**, a popular resort to the west, has sandy beaches and the remains of a temple dedicated to **Poseidon** and **Amphitrite**.

Inland, free of mass tourism, whitewashed villages pepper the hillsides. The intricately decorated, two-storeyed *Peristerouias* (dovecotes) are a distinctive feature with some 1300 dotted around the island. On **Mt Examboúrgo** are the remains of the former Ionian capital and an impressive Venetian fortress built from the ancient city's stone.

Thíra (Santoríni)

PÁROS, NÁXOS, IOS

Mavropétra

Oía
Finikiá

AEGEAN SEA

Potamós
Manólas
Agrília
Thirassía

Skaros
Imerovígli
Firostéfani

Skála Firá   **Firá**

Nea Kaméni

Karterádos   Monólithos

Palia Kaméni

Messaría   Vothon
Exo Gonia

Aspronisi

Athinos

Órmos Athinos   Pirgos   Episkopí

Megalochori   566 m   Kamarí
Monastery

Akrotíri   Ancient Thíra
Embório   Périssa

Akrotíri Ruins

0   4 km
0   2 miles

N

CRETE

The Cyclades at a Glance

BEST TIMES TO VISIT

Most visitors flood the islands from **June** to **September** to enjoy the perfect weather. **May** and **October** are warm, largely crowd-free months. Winters are mild with some stormy days and travelling may be hampered by high seas.

GETTING THERE

In summer **Mýkonos** is served by frequent international **charter flights**. There are also internal flights between Athens and the islands with airports. **Mýkonos**–Athens (4-8 daily), Crete (Iráklion), Rhodes, Thíra (3-4 weekly), Chíos, Mytilíni (Lésbos), Sámos (1–2 weekly). **Mílos**–Athens (2–4 daily and 1 in winter). **Náxos**–Athens (3–5 daily). **Páros**–Athens (daily up to 8 in summer – 5 in winter). **Thíra**–Athens, Crete, Mýkonos, Rhodes (daily). **Sýros**–Athens (2–3 daily). Ferry lines from Piraeus to islands and between islands. **Amorgós** in summer there are daily links to Náxos, Herákliá, Schinoússa Koufoníssi (daily) and Donoússa (5 per week). **Amorgós** to Piraeus 5 daily via Náxos, Páros, Sýros; 6 daily with Tínos; 8 with Mýkonos. Other links: Astipálaia, Thíra, Mílos and Náfplion. Hydrofoil weekly to Herákliá, Schinoússa Koufoníssi, Thíra, Íos, Náxos, Páros Mýkonos, Tínos and Sýros. **Port Authority**, tel: (0285) 71-259. **Anáfi** links twice weekly with

Piraeus via Thíra, Íos, Náxos, and Páros. Amorgós and Sýros (1 weekly). Catamarans in summer to other Cyclades islands and Piraeus. **Port Authority**, tel: (0286) 61-216. **Andros** daily to Rafina, Tínos, Mýkonos (also Sýros less frequently). With Dodecanese via Páros, Náxos, Kos and Rhodes (3 weekly) and Astipálaia, Kálimnos and Amorgós (1 weekly). **Port Authority**, tel: (0282) 22-250. **Antíparos** hourly from Paros: caique from Paroikiá; car ferry from Poúnta. **Port Authority**, tel: (0284) 61-485. **Délos** is served by tourist boats from Mýkonos, Tínos, Náxos and Páros. **Donoússa** (Back Island) from Náxos and Amorgós. **Folégandros** ferries to Piraeus, Íos, Thíra and Síkinos (5 weekly) also Mílos, Sífnos, Sérifos, Kýthnos (several) and weekly with Kímolos, Crete, Kássos, Kárpathos Chálki, Náxos, Páros, Sými and Rhodes plus excursions from Íos. **Port Authority**, tel: (0286) 41-249. **Herákliá** (Back Island) day trips from Rhodes or Náxos. **Íos** ferries daily to Piraeus and all major Cyclades, 5 weekly to Crete, 1 weekly to Thessaloníki. Excursions to Thíra, Páros, Náxos, Mýkonos, Folégandros and Síkinos. **Port Authority**, tel: (0286) 91-264. **Kéa** daily ferry with Lavrion, 2 weekly with Kýthnos and Sýros. Hydrofoil daily in summer from Kýthnos, Piraeus (Zea).

Hydrofoil from **Kéa** to Rafína, Milos, Sífnos, Sérifos, Kýthnos and Kímolos. **Port Authority**, tel: (0288) 21-344. **Kéros** (Back Island) day trip from Koufoníssi. **Kímolos** 3 weekly with Piraeus on Western Line, weekly with Folégandros, Síkinos, Íos and Thíra. 3 daily water taxis to Milos. Hydrofoil weekly to Rafína, Milos, Sífnos, Sérifos, Kýthnos, Kéa. **Port Authority**, tel: (0287) 51-332. **Koufoníssi** (Back Island) from Náxos and Amorgós. Port Authority, tel: (0285) 71-375. **Kýthnos** daily ferries with Piraeus and islands on same line. 2–3 weekly with Lavrion (Kímolos, Folégandros, Síkinos, Íos and Thíra). **Port Authority**, tel: (0281) 32-290. **Milos** ferries from Piraeus 6 per week and 2–3 a week with Crete, 3 weekly to Folégandros and 2 weekly to Rhodes (Kárpathos, Chálki, Sými). 1 weekly with Amorgós and Thíra. **Port Authority**, tel: (0287) 22-100. **Mýkonos** daily ferry links with Piraeus, Rafína, Andros, Tínos, Sýros, Páros, Náxos, Íos and Thíra. Several per week with Crete (Iráklion), Sámos, Amorgós, Kos, Rhodes and Back Islands. 2 weekly with Síkinos, Folégandros, Skiáthos and Thessaloníki. 1 weekly with Kálimnos, Sífnos, Sérifos, Níssyros, Tílos and Ikaría. Hydrofoil daily to Náxos and Rafína via Andros and Tínos. Trips to Délos daily. **Port**

The Cyclades at a Glance

Authority, tel: (0289) 22-218.
Náxos daily ferries to Piraeus (also Páros, Sýros, Ios, Thíra, Mýkonos, Tínos, Andros). Daily boat to Amorgós via Back Islands. 3 weekly links with Crete (Iráklion), Sífnos, Sérifos, Sámos, Ikaría and Rafína. 2 weekly links with Síkinos and Folégandros. Hydrofoil daily (except Sunday) to Rafína (via Mýkonos, Tínos, Andros). **Port Authority**, tel: (0285) 22-300.
Páros daily ferry links with Sýros and Piraeus, Náxos, Mýkonos, Ios, Thíra, Crete (Iráklion) and Sífnos. 3–4 weekly connections with Rafína, Sámos, Ikaría, Kárpathos, Rhodes and Amorgós. Also weekly with Corfu and Ancona in summer. Frequent boats to Antíparos from Paroikiá and Poúnta in Páros. Hydrofoil connections with Náxos, Mýkonos,Ios, Thíra, Tínos, Sýros, Amorgós and Piraeus. **Port Authority**, tel: (0284) 21-240.
Schinoússa (Back Island) from Náxos and Amorgós.
Sérifos daily ferry connections to Piraeus via Kýthnos and Milos via Sífnos. 4 weekly to Kímolos, 3 weekly to Thíra and Folégandros, 2 weekly with Síkinos and Ios. Weekly to Sýros. **Port Authority**, tel: (0281) 51-470.
Sífnos daily ferry connections to Piraeus via Kýthnos and Milos via Sérifos. 4 weekly to Kímolos, 2–3 weekly to Thíra Folégandros and Síkinos and Ios. Weekly to Páros, Crete,

Rhodes, Kárpathos, Kássos, Chálki, and Sými. **Port Authority**, tel: (0284) 31-617.
Síkinos 5 ferries per week to Piraeus, 4 weekly to Thíra, several per week to Páros, Náxos, Sífnos, Sérifos and Sýros. Weekly to Kýthnos, Kímolos, Crete and Dodecanese. **Port Authority**, tel: (0286) 51-222.
Sýros daily with Piraeus, Mýkonos, Tínos Páros, Náxos and Amorgós. 4–5 weekly with Rafína, Andros, Thíra, Ios. 3 weekly to Síkinos and Folégandros. 2 weekly to Astipálaia and Back Islands, 1 weekly to Ikaría, Sámos and Anáfi. Daily catamaran to Piraeus and other Cyclades. **Port Authority**, tel: (0281) 82-690.
Thíra daily ferry connections with Piraeus, Ios, Páros, Náxos, Mýkonos and Crete (Iráklion), 2–3 weekly with Dodecanese, Skiáthos and Thessaloníki. Frequent connections with other Cyclades (also catamarans). Thirasia daily from Thíra. **Port Authority**, tel: (0286) 22-239.
Tínos daily ferry connections with Piraeus, Mýkonos, Sýros, Andros and Rafína. 6 weekly with Páros, 5 weekly with Amorgós, 3 weekly

Dodecanese and Thíra. 2 weekly Crete, Ios, Skiáthos, Thessaloníki and Back Islands. (see page 124 for on-line timetable and booking).

WHERE TO STAY

(see At a Glance p. 113).

WHERE TO EAT

(see At a Glance p. 113).

USEFUL CONTACTS

Tourist Police:
Amorgós, tel: (0285) 71-210.
Andros, tel: (0282) 22-300.
Folégandros, tel: (0286) 41-249.
Ios, tel: (0286) 91-222.
Kéa (Tzía), tel: (0288) 21-100.
Kímolos, tel: (0287) 51-205.
Koufoníssi, tel: (0285) 71-375.
Kýthnos, tel: (0281) 31-201.
Milos, tel: (0287) 21-204.
Mýkonos, tel: (0289) 22-482.
Náxos, tel: (0285) 22-100.
Páros, tel: (0284) 23-333.
Antíparos, tel: (0284) 61-202.
Thíra (Santoríni), tel: (0286) 22-649.
Sérifos, tel: (0281) 51-300.
Sífnos, tel: (0284) 31-210.
Sýros, tel: (0281) 22-610.
Tínos, tel: (0283) 22-255.
Délos Archaeological Site tel: (0289) 22-259.

CYCLADES	J	F	M	A	M	J	J	A	S	O	N	D
AVERAGE TEMP. °F	52	52	55	61	68	75	79	77	73	66	59	54
AVERAGE TEMP. °C	11	11	13	16	20	24	26	25	23	19	15	12
HOURS OF SUN DAILY	5	5	6	7	10	11	12	11	9	7	5	4
RAINFALL ins.	2.5	2	2	1	0.5	0	0	0	0	1.5	2	3
RAINFALL mm	66	52	47	18	10	3	1	2	6	36	47	70
DAYS OF RAINFALL	14	11	10	7	4	1	1	1	2	6	9	14

6
The Ionian Islands

The Greek name for the Ionian Islands – *Eptanisi* (eptá = seven) – refers directly to the seven islands: **Corfu** (Kérkyra), **Ithaca** (Itháki), **Kefaloniá**, **Kýthira**, **Lefkáda** (Lefkás), **Paxí** (Páxos) and **Zákinthos** (Zante).

Six of these share a common history, architecture and culture but the seventh, **Kýthera**, is a political rather than geographical inclusion, isolated from the rest at the easternmost tip of the Peloponnese. A higher rainfall and hot, often humid summers create some of the greenest of the Greek island landscapes dotted with olive groves, cypress trees and sparkling spring flowers. A summer haze takes the harshness off the light and the whole effect is Italianate. The islands retain a strong individuality: **Corfu** is a popular international tourist destination yet there is still much left to discover. The best beaches are found on **Zákinthos** and their popularity has been to the detriment of nesting turtles. Although a causeway connects **Lefkáda** with the mainland it has escaped tourist development. **Meganísi**, a spectacular and wild islet, lies off the east coast of Lefkáda. **Paxí** is like one large olive grove and is a rural idyll, whereas tiny **Antípaxi** with sandy beaches offers solitude. **Kefaloniá**, the largest of the islands and only recently 'discovered' has a wild, unspoiled mountain landscape and high cliffs. **Itháki**, with its small fishing villages and connections with Odysseus, is undeveloped.

There are numerous smaller islands – **Othoní**, **Eríkousa** and **Mathráki**, **Elafónissos** … some just mountains in the Ionian sea, reached from the larger islands by caique or ferries calling en route in the high season.

DON'T MISS

*** **Corfu:** the Venetian town with streets which never fail to delight.
*** **Zákinthos:** the views of islands and mainland from the summit of Mt Skopós.
** **Kefaloniá:** walks through the forest on Mt Aínos.
** **Lefkáda:** the superb beaches of the east coast.
* **Paxí:** the sea caves on the west coast and Antípaxi islet.

Opposite: *Vlachérna is joined to the Konóni peninsula on Corfu by a causeway and Mouse Island sits just offshore.*

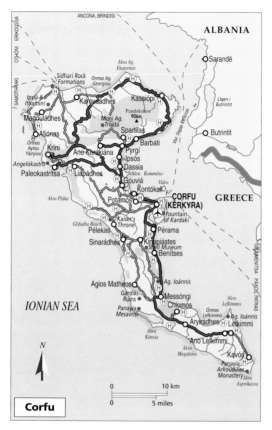

ANCONA, BRINDISI
ALBANIA
OTHONI ERIKOUSSA
SAMOTHRAKI
Akra Ag.
Ekaterinis
Sarandë
Sidhari Rock
Formations
Ormos Ag.
Georgiou
Ipsili &
Itrhamini
Karousádhes
Kassiópi
Llqen i
Butrintit
Pandokrator
906m
Butrinti
Magouládhes
Moni Ag.
Triada
Spartilas
Pavia
Afiónas
Ormos
Ayiou
Yioryiou
Krini
Ano Korakiána
Barbáti
Pyrgí
Ipsós
Dassia
Angelókastro
Akra Komméno
Paleokastritsa
Liapádhes
Gouviá
Vidos
Kontókali
Akra Pláka
Potamós
CORFU
(KÉRKYRA)
GREECE
Kaiser's
Throne
Fountain
of Kardaki
Glifadha Beach
Pélekas
Pérama
Sinarádhes
Kinopiástes
Shell Museum
Benítses
Agios Matheos
Ag. Ioánnis
IONIAN SEA
Gardiki
Ruins
Messóngi
Chlomós
Akra
Lefkímmis
Panayia
Mesavrísi
Ormos
Lefkímmis
Ag. Ioánnis
Akra
Kónsia
Arylrádhes
Lefkimmi
Ano Lefkímmi
Akra
Megahóro
Kavós
Panayia
Arkoudilas
Monastery
Akra
Asprókavos
IGOUMENITSA   PAXOS   PATRAS
Vor. Steno Kerkiras

N

0   10 km
0   5 miles

Corfu

CORFU (KERKYRA) ***

Countless thousands of people have been 'turned on' to Greek islands after a visit to Corfu. Homer called it the happy isle – *Scheria* – and thanks to Lawrence Durrell's eulogy (and perhaps the fact that cricket is played there) it became a adopted home for expatriate 'Brits'.

This lush island (area 592km²; 229 sq miles) with idyllic beaches retains its beauty in spite of its popularity and the friendliness of Corfiots is still a matter of national pride.

Kérkyra (**Corfu town**) is both the largest, most attractive capital in the **Ionian** islands and has a bustling, cosmopolitan atmosphere and wealth of architectural treasures. For aimless wandering on foot or in horse-drawn *monippo*, the old town is unbeatable.

The Venetians began to set out the town in the 14th century when the Mediaeval town on **Cape Sidáro** (the site of the old Venetian Fortress) was bursting at its seams. The **Campiello** was constructed first with narrow streets where the upper storeys of the houses are almost touching. Later building styles show a more open 'Renaissance' approach with numerous small squares. Under British rule the town expanded again: the Venetian town walls were dismantled and elegant Georgian buildings erected.

The crumbling **Old Fort** (Paleó Froúrio), begun in Byzantine times and much modified since, has a sound

Opposite: *Typical of Corfu town's elegance is Guildford Street with the town hall square.*

CLIMATE

The islands off the west coast of the mainland are greener and more lush than other islands because rainfall is high, but the climate is still Mediterranean: summers are warm but there is often a hint of haze about the skies. In spring and summer the Sirocco blows but here it is humid having collected moisture from the sea. A winter wind of moist Atlantic air brings dark skies and heavy squalls in the Ionian islands.

and light show most evenings (open daily 08:00–19:00). The **New Fort** (Néo Froúrio), built after a Turkish attack in 1576, was a Greek naval base until recently (open daily 09:00–21:00) – its bastions offer a view over the old town and its moat contains the town market.

The area immediately west of the old fort, **Spianáda** (Esplanade), was developed under Napoleonic rule and nowadays cricket is played here. The **Listón**, a lengthy row of arcaded cafés on the western edge is modelled on the Rue de Rivoli in Paris – the local tipple is *tsintsi bira* (ginger beer). The **Palace of St Michael and St George** at the northern

CHURCH INDEX
A. Agios Spiridonas
B. Panayia ton Xenon
C. Agios Ioánnis
D. Agios Peteres
E. Panayia Tenedou
F. Anglican Church
G. Greek Orthodox Cathedral

Above: *Old buildings with their shuttered windows are a well-preserved feature of Venetian rule.*
Opposite: *Undoubtedly popular but scenically superb – Paleokastrítsa is a favourite destination.*

ODYSSEUS' FOOTSTEPS

The islanders of **Ithaca** have made great play of their links, however tenuous or fanciful, with Odysseus, son of Laertes and Anticleia. West of Váthi at **Marmaróspilia** is the Cave of the Nymphs and at **Dexiá** a sleeping Odysseus was carried ashore by the Phaeacians. Disguised as a beggar Odysseus met swineherd Eumaeus at **Ellinikó**.

North of Váthi at **Aetós** is the so-called Castle of Odysseus; at Agrós is the Field of Laertes.

---

end houses the **Museum of Asiatic Art** (open Tuesday–Sunday 08:00–14:30). It is a short step west into the **Campiello** with the **Orthodox Cathedral** (1577) and **Byzantine Museum** (open Monday–Saturday 08:45–15:00; Sunday 09:30–14:30). The church of Corfu's patron saint **Agios Spirídon** keeps his aged bones in a silver reliquary and locals pray to the saint as a healer.

The **Archaeological Museum** is sited in **Garítsa** – the Corinthian monumental scultpures are superb and one whole room is reserved for the massive Gorgon pediment uncovered near the **Temple of Artemis** (585BC) in Kanóni (open Tuesday–Sunday 08:30–15:00). The small town beach, **Mon Repos**, takes its name from the royal villa and park above it.

North of **Kérkyra** (Corfu town) the sweeping bay has been developed to cater for sun and sea holidays with every conceivable form of water sport available. The strip begins with **Kontokáli**; **Gouviá** overlooking a lagoon has a Venetian arsenal and marina; **Cape Komméno's** beaches are nothing to write home about but **Dassiá** has a beach fringed with olive trees. Former fishing villages of **Ipsós** and **Pirgí** mark the ends of the island's 'golden mile' and to the north there is a quiet haven in the shape of small coves and beaches offering brief respite before **Barbáti**.

Kassiópi along the north coast is a bustling resort. It has four small beaches that can be reached by walking on paths from the headland. Above the village stands a ruined Byzantine fortress on a site rich in historical memories since there was a Hellenistic town here and then a Roman settlement visited by both Cicero and Nero. A half hour's walk from Kassiópi, along the cliffs to the south brings you to some lovely beaches: **Avláki**, **Kouyévinas** and then further west, **Kalamáki**, with its grey sands and views across to **Albania**.

Paleokastrítsa in the northwest is a paradise in spring time: from here and **Lákones**, just to the northeast, are some excellent walks to **Kríni** and the wild ruins of **Angelókastro** which is situated on top of the crag.

The southern coast closest to Corfu town has seen the worst tourist excesses – **Benítses**, once a pretty village, has been changed beyond recognition by development but **Moraítika** and **Messóngi** are not far behind. With a little planning you can leave the worst of the crowds behind by heading towards the far south to the beach of **Agios Górdhis** with about 2km (3⅓ miles) of golden sands, or to **Tria Avlákia**, **Paramónas** and **Skithi**. A long stretch of sand dunes separates **Límni Korissíon** lagoon from the sea – this is the best place on the island to see the spring and autumn migratory birds. **Kavós** at the southern tip is a 'bop till you drop' resort.

ITHACA (ITHÁKI) **

Itháki is traditionally the island of Odysseus, Homer's peripatetic hero. Two mountainous peninsulas joined by an isthmus comprise the 96km² (37 sq miles) island: roads are few and many islanders travel by caique between coastal villages.

Váthi, the capital, is at the end of a wooded bay with an islet just off shore. It was rebuilt in traditional style after the earthquake in 1953; two ruined French forts (**Loútsa** and **Kástro**) stand either side of the harbour entrance. An icon of Christ in the **Church of the Taxiárchos** is claimed to be the work of the young El Greco (*see* p. 25). The **Archaeology Museum** has a local collection of classical and Mycenaean objects (open Tuesday–Sunday 08:30–14:30). From the harbour there are caique services to good beaches at **Bímata**, **Filiatró**, **Skinós** and **Sarakinikó**.

MT PANTOKRATOR

Mt Pantokrátor (900m; 2953ft) has always been a special draw for visiting naturalists. A road climbs from the coast via a series of hairpin bends to **Spartílas**, **Strinílas** and then **Petália**. From Petália, there is a bumpy road to **Perithía** which is largely deserted. The path to the summit of the mountain takes an hour from the village.

CORFU'S TINY INLETS

Since Corfu is a year-round holiday island it is often possible to reach the three completely unspoiled islets of **Othoní** (the largest), **Erikousa** (beautiful beach) and **Mathráki** (turtles) even outside high summer.

Caiques run from Sidari and in summer from Agios Stéfanos. Ferries run from Corfu town and there are rooms to rent.

Right: *Villagers in Kefaloniá have a love affair with flowers. The cottages near Marko reflect this.*
Below: *Idyllic Fiskárdo has become a favourite with yachtsmen exploring the beautiful islands.*

KEFALONIÁ CAVES

Sámi has become the main ferry port of Kefaloniá and a growing resort – the attraction is the marvellous caves. **Melissáni cave**, once a sanctuary of the God Pau, has an indoor lake dappled in shades of blue as filtered light from a hole in the roof plays on it. Near the village of Chaliotáta, the **Drogkaráti cave** is big enough to hold concerts in, with a brightly lit wonderland of stalactites and stalagmites.

KEFALONIÁ ★★★

The wild rugged beauty of Kefaloniá, the largest Ionian island (area 781km²; 301 sq miles), has been appreciated for years by walkers but few package tours operate there.

Signs of earliest habitation date from 50,000BC and in Classical times there were four city states (**Sámi, Pali, Krani** and **Pronnoi**). In the Byzantine era it endured the attentions of Arab raiders followed by Normans, Venetians and a brief period of Turkish rule (1483–1504) before reverting to the Venetians.

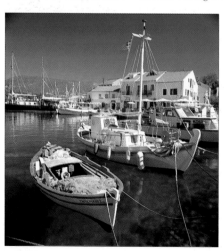

Argostóli, an unprepossessing capital in a superb setting, was reduced to rubble in a series of earthquakes in 1953. The **Drapanós** bridge with its low arches survived and leads to the **Lassí peninsula** with a few sandy beaches and two swallow holes at **Katovóthres** where, prior to the earthquake the tidal race was strong enough to provide electrical power. An impressive lighthouse (**Agios Theódori**) sits at the peninsula tip. Ancient **Kráni**, southeast of the capital, is a wild, unkempt site with remains of Cyclopean walls and a **Temple to Demeter**.

The larger **Palíki peninsula** reached by ferry from **Argostóli** has a scattering of pretty villages and very good sandy beaches at **Agios Spyrídon**, **Michalitsáta**, **Lépeda** and **Xi**; the port of **Lixoúri** has become the island's second city.

Ferries to **Itháki** and **Astakós** use Agia Evfimía which is a much prettier port than Sámi and a good base for exploration of the north. By day the fishing village of **Asos** offers panoramic views and an impressive Venetian fortress from which to watch the sunset before sampling the lively

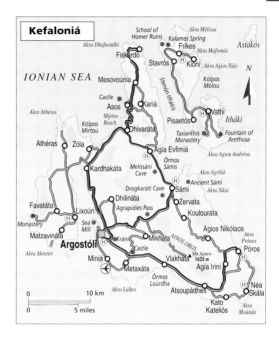

Greek nightlife. The village of **Fiskárdo**, now popular with the yachting fraternity, survived the 1953 earthquake intact and some of its exquisite old house are available for rental.

The bulk of **Mt Aínos** provides shelter for the south coast's sandy beaches and a number of resorts have been established along this stretch. **Skála** has a long beach and nearby Roman Villa; **Lourdáta** gets crowded but has a nature trail which is quite spectacular for its flowers in spring while **Ratzaklí** near **Potomákia** plays host to nesting loggerhead turtles protected by volunteers.

KÝTHIRA **

With the cutting of the Corinth canal, Kýthira lost its status as a link between the Aegean and Ionian seas. Although its historical ties are with the Ionian Islands, geographically it is part of the Peloponnese. This unspoiled island (area 278km²; 107 sq miles) shares a claim with Cyprus to be the birthplace of **Aphrodite**.

KEFALONIA WINES

The Venetians introduced the **Robóla** grape variety in the 13th century and the islanders produced distinctive and highly regarded dry whites with a fragrant citrus 'nose'. Since 1978 modern techniques have been used to produce wines a world apart from what is generally on offer in Greece. Try the pale dry **Gentili Animus** (100% Robóla) or **Gentili Fume** (Robóla aged in oak casks). Calligas produce **Thiniatikó** – a velvet smooth port wine as well as **Amando** – a fortified Muscat dessert wine. **Tsoussi** is a white wine made from a grape unique to Kefaloniá.

Kýthira
Platia Ammos
Agia Pelagiá
Potamós • Palio Chora
Diakofti
Agia Arondika
Sophia Cave
Temple of Aphrodite Avlemonas
Milopótamos
Paliopolis
Fratsia
Mirtidióti Monastery
Kýthira Kapsáli
N
0 5 km
0 3 miles

LEFKÁDA'S BEACHES

Although the west coast is rugged some superb beaches nestle beneath the cliffs at **Pevkóulia**, **Kathísma** and **Kalamítsi**. At the southern tip lies **Kávo tis Kyrás** (lady's cape) from whence a distraught Sappho, rejected by Phaon, is supposed to have thrown herself. Nearby **Vassilíki** is regarded as heaven by windsurfers.

Chóra, the capital, is a breathtakingly pretty village of whitewashed houses set high above the port of **Kapsáli**. The **Venetian kástro** (castle or fort) is a ruin but the town still has 10 Venetian mansions displaying their coats of arms. Kapsáli with its fine beaches is also the island's main resort – just inland at **Livádi** is an incongruous British built 'viaduct' and to the west the dramatically set **Monastery of Panayía Mirtidíon**. Near **Milopótamos**, known for an unusual number of streams that flow in and around the village, lies **Káto** which is a deserted Venetian town. From here, paths lead to a sandy cove at **Limiónas** and a cave at **Agia Sofía** which has frescoes painted on its walls.

Most ferry traffic comes to **Agia Pelagía** but as a base **Potamós** is both more attractive and better appoint-ed with a large Sunday market. Nearby **Palío Chóra** is a wonderfully atmospheric place – a deserted Byzantine town high above an abyss into which frantic mothers once threw their children and then themselves to avoid capture by Barbarossa, the brutal Byzantine pirate.

ANTIKYTHIRA *
Antikythira is a dusty, wind-buffeted rock with two tiny hamlets. The island lies betweeen Crete and the Peloponnese and ferries call just once a week.

ELAFÓNISSOS *
Caiques travel daily to Elafónissos from **Agia Pelágia** or **Neápolis** (mainland) in the high season. There is a single village devoted to fishing (with a couple of pensions) and a pair of pristine white sand beaches at **Katá Nísso**.

LEFKÁDA (LEFKAS) *
Colonists from ancient Corinth dug the canal which separates the 'island' from the mainland. Earthquakes hit Lefkáda town badly in 1948 and in 1953 – modern buildings collapsed, though **Santa Maura**, the old Frankish castle next to the channel, and the 18th-century churches (**Agios Minás**, **Agios Dimítrios**, **Agios Spirídon** and **Pantokrátor**) fared better. Houses were rebuilt with

stone ground floors and 'anti seismic' sheet metal walls
to the upper floors. The lagoon next to Santa Maura is a
magnet for migratory birds – heron species, pelican and
innumerable waders. The town's museums are well
worth visiting, particularly the **Orpheus Folklore
Museum** with a display of exquisite local embroidery
and old maps (open daily 10:00–13:00 and 18:00–21:00).
Traditional embroidery is obtainable in several mountain villages – try **Karyá** where there is also a museum
(**Museum Maria Koutsochéro**) and **Englouví**, the lentil
capital of Lefkáda.

Most tourist development has taken place along the
gentle east coast – **Nidrí** is the busiest resort with tiny
wooded (and privately owned) islets of **Mandourí**,
Sparti Skorpídi and **Skórpios**. There is a pleasant walk
inland to the village of **Rachí** which has a spring, usually
reduced to a mere trickle in summer. To the south there
is a good sandy beach at **Dessími** and a pretty pebble
beach at **Póros**.

MEGANÍSI **

Rocky Meganísi (area 23km²; 9 sq
miles), lying off the southeast coast
of **Lefkáda**, is a spectacular day
excursion from Nidrí. **Váthi**, the
port, has excellent fish tavernas
but accommodation is limited. A
sea cave – **Papanikólaos Grotto** –
is included on the excursion route.
The popular **Festival of Agios
Konstantinos** brings crowds to the
island on 21 May.

In high season boats from Nidrí
also travel east of Meganísi to
Kálamos and **Kástos**, little more
than mountains in the sea. The
easiest way to approach the islands
is from **Mítikas** on the mainland:
Kástos was once known for its wine;
Kálamos survives on fishing.

> ### SEA CAVES
>
> There are seven caves hidden
> among the sheer limestone
> cliffs off the west coast of
> Paxí that can be visited by
> local boat trips. **Grammatíko**
> is the biggest, **Ípapanti** is
> traditionally Homer's wild
> cove and cave, **Kastanítha**
> has a roof 185m (067ft) high
> and **Orthólithos** is guarded
> by a monolith at its entrance.
> A natural 'bridge' (*Tripitos*)
> at the **Moúsmouli Cliffs**
> is another feature that is
> visible from the sea.

Below: *Fishing and the
inevitable net mending is
still a family occupation on
Lefkáda and other islands.*

ZAKINTHOS' BEACHES

Loggerhead turtles (*see* p. 11) were first to recognize the clear water and fine expanse of sand of **Laganás** long before beach umbrellas, cafés, discos or tavernas. It is possible to escape the crowds at **Pórto Zóro** and **Banana Beach** where the sands are full of white sea daffodils in high summer. Further towards the peninsula tip are excellent beaches at **Gérakas**, **Daphní** and **Sekánika**.
  The tiny offshore islet of **Marathoníssi** has a good beach and is popular with day trippers.

PAXÍ (PAXOS) **

Although Paxí is the smallest of the main Ionian islands (area 23km²; 9 sq miles) it possesses abundant charm. Dramatic limestone cliffs on its west coast fade to low hills on the east and in places the island seems to be a silver-sea of olive trees.

Gáios, the miniature capital with wonderfully narrow streets, takes its name from a disciple of St Paul who brought Christianity to the island. Its Venetian fortress, **Kástro Agios Nikólaos** (built in 1423), sits with an old windmill on an islet facing the harbour: **Panayía** and **Mongoníssi** are two nearby islets, connected by boat.

Boats from Corfu call at **Lákka** with its distinctive brown and indigo houses; just outside the village is the **Church of Ipapanti** with an onion dome. At **Grammatikoú** there is a fortified Venetian mansion complete with a tower.

ANTÍPAXI **

Four or five caiques daily leave **Gáios** in the main holiday season (June–September) for tiny Antípaxi which has superb beaches with fine sand at **Voutoúmi** and **Vríka**. The island is renowned for its wines and every available metre is covered with well-tended vines.

Below: *Bustling Zákinthos town with its street cafés shows no traces of the earthquake which decimated it in 1953.*

ZÁKINTHOS (ZANTE) ***

The Venetians referred to fertile Zákinthos as their 'flower of the east' but since then the islanders have cashed in on mass tourism and, in season, more discerning (and frequently higher spending) folk are tending to look elsewhere.

Near the town hall in **Platía Solomoú**, the neo-Byzantine museum has a superb collection of Ionian art rescued from churches

including work by Michael Damskinós, the icon painter who taught El Greco (open Tuesday–Sunday 08:00–14:30). The **Bocháli District** with its mansions was once favoured by wealthy Venetians – a cobbled path leads to the **Venetian Kástro** (open daily 08:00–20:00).

Mt Skopós which dominates the peninsula can be climbed via a road leading from **Argássi** – in spring the route is ablaze with wildflowers (a dozen and more species of wild orchid included).

The track to the summit passes the ruined 11th-century church of **Agios Nikólaos Megalomátis** which has a mosaic floor constructed over the site of an earlier **Temple of Artemis**. The white church of **Panayía Skopiótissa** stands proud on the summit and the views over the island and the Peloponnese mainland are superb.

Above: *Trips to the Blue Grotto are popular with visitors to Zákinthos.*

The north coast road out of Zakínthos town passes the Kryonéri Fountain, once used for watering Venetian ships, and then brings you to a series of beaches – **Tsilví**, **Plános Ampoula** on to **Alikanás** and around the headland to **Alikés** .

The west coast, rugged and white, contrasts strongly with the rest of the island and most people see it by caique or on foot. There is a wrecked ship near **Porto Vrómi** and a host of sea-sculpted features – the finest is **Kianoún cave**, a 'blue' grotto best viewed in the early morning light.

The Ionian Islands at a Glance

Winters can be quite cold and damp with heavy storms. **Spring**, from **March–May** brings many flowers into bloom – Corfu, Zákinthos and Kefaloniá are particularly resplendent. Crowds start building up when the weather becomes hot roughly late **June–September**. **October** is crowd free, the sea is warm and the air is clean.

Bus connections in Athens run from the 100 Kifissíou terminal (take bus #051 from Omónia Square to reach it) and serve the west coast (Corfu, Kefaloniá, Lefkás and Patrás for Ionian isles). Corfu is served by **scheduled flights** from many European cities, several flights daily from Athens and numerous seasonal **charter flights** from the UK. SEEA, a Greek airline, offers flights between Athens and London (2 Moustoxídi Street, Athens, tel: (01) 46-241). Daily flights from Athens to Kefaloniá and Zákinthos and inter-island flights about three times a week. Contact Olympic Airways in Corfu town (20 Kapodistríou, tel: (0661) 38-694/5/6). **Lefkáda** has two daily flights from Athens and charters in summer from the UK. **Kýthira** is served by at least one flight daily from Athens – Kýthira airport information, tel: (0735) 33-292; tickets from Olympic (49

Elefethería Venizélou, Pótamos: tel (0735) 33-362). For **island hopping** by sea – between June and September ferries operate most days from Pátras to Brindisi (18hours) and vice-versa with stops en route: **Pátras**, **Kefaloniá** (Argostóli), **Itháki**, **Paxí**, **Corfu**, **Brindisi**. Hourly services between **Igoumenítsa** and **Corfu** (2 hours). Ferries sail from Igoumenítsa (reduced winter schedule) and in season there are connections with Itháki, Kefaloniá and Pátras.Regular year-round ferries from Italian ports of Ancona, Bari, Brindisi (also from Trieste and Ortona). A free stopover on a particular island is usually allowed if specified in advance. A cata- maran links Corfu with Brindisi (3hr 30min), tickets bookable from Corfu: Charitos Travel, 35 Arseníou Street, tel: (0661) 44-611 or Athens – 28 Nikis, Sýntagma, tel: (01) 322-0503. Ferries (twice-weekly) link Corfu with Eríkousa, Othoní and Mathráki. **Port Authority Corfu**, tel (0661) 32-655. **Kefaloniá** and **Itháki** are served by many of the same boats: daily ferries link Pátras (5hr 30min), with Itháki (Váthi) and Kefaloniá (Sámi): Ferries from Astakós (mainland) travel daily to Itháki (Váthi and Píso Aetós) and on to Kefaloniá (Agia Eufimía). Seasonal ferries connect Kefaloniá (Fiskárdo) with Itháki (both Frikés and Vassilikí); Kefaloniá (Póros and Argostóli) with Kilíni

(Peloponnese); Kefaloniá (Pessáda) with Zákinthos (Skinári).**Hydrofoils** run in summer from Sámi to Váthi and to Zákinthos from Kefaloniá (Póros and Argostóli). **Port Authority Kefaloniá**, tel: (0671) 22-224, **Itháki**, tel: (0674) 32-209. **Kýthira** ferries link with mainland: daily to Neápoli, 5 weekly to Gythion, 2 weekly to Monemvássia, Piraeus and Crete (Kastelli), 1 weekly to Antikythira. In summer hydrofoil services connect Agia Pelagia in Kýthira with Gythion (5 weekly) and 3 weekly with Piraeus, Hydra, Spétses and Monemvássia. **Port Autority Kýthira**, tel: (0735) 33-280. In summer ferries run from Nidrí and Vassilikí, (two ports in **Lefkáda**), to Kefaloniá (Sámi, Fiskárdo and Póros) – also daily from Nidrí to Meganísi (Váthi). **Port Authority Lefkáda,** tel: (0645) 92-509). **Paxí** (Páxos) is served year- round by twice-weekly car ferry from Corfu (3 hours) call- ing at Sívota on the mainland (contact Sívota Travel on Corfu, tel: (0665) 93-222). Between June and September there are daily caiques from Corfu (3 hours) and Parga (2 hours) and hydrofoils from Igoumenítsa, Préveza and Lefkáda. **Port Authority Paxí**, (0662) 32-259. **Zákinthos** (Zante) 6 to 7 daily from Kilíni (mainland), 1 to 2

from Kefaloniá (Pessáda); also daily from Kefaloniá to Skinári. Hydrofoils in season from Zákinthos town to Kefaloniá (Póros and Argostóli) and the mainland (Pátras and Pírgos).
Port Authority Zákinthos, tel: (0695) 42-417.
MINOR ISLANDS
Antíkythira weekly stop by boats between Kýthira and Crete – *meltémi* permitting.
Elafoníssos daily caique in summer from Neápolis (Peloponnese) and Agia Pelagía (Kýthira).
Eríkousa, **Mathráki**, **Othoní** a twice weekly 'circular' car ferry runs from Corfu town to Eríkousa, Mathráki, Othoní, and back. There are also excursion boats.
Kálamos is served regularly from mainland (Mítikas) and by occasional boats from Kefaloniá (Sámi), Itháki, Nidri (Lefkáda) and Meganísi.
Kástos irregular connections – hired caique is the only reliable option. (Kálamos and Kástos are islets east of Meganísi).
Meganisi regular crossing from Nidri (port of Lefkáda).

GETTING AROUND

Bus services are regular on **Corfu** and **Zákinthos** but become progressively more limited on the smaller islands with no more than one or two services a day linking towns on **Lefkáda**, **Kefalonía** and **Kýthira**. On all islands **taxis** are a cheap and comfortable way of making trips; remote

beaches can be reached by caique service in season. (*see* page 124 for on-line timetable and booking).

WHERE TO STAY

Outside the main season there is little difficulty in finding accommodation on spec in hotels and pensions although many smaller establishments close in winter. Low season prices are about two-thirds those of the summer months. During July and August advance booking is essential: the EOT in Athens has comprehensive lists of all hotels and pensions with classification and rates. Details of rooms to rent can be obtained from the Tourist Police.
Itháki – accommodation is limited outside Váthi. On **Kefaloniá** hotels are scattered around the coastal resorts together with reasonable numbers of rooms for rent.
Kýthira is not well-blessed with hotels and there are comparatively few rooms to rent.
Lefkáda's accommodation tends to be on the east coast south of Lefkáda town. Most hotel accommodation on **Paxí** is pre-booked – rooms are

better value and plentiful.
Zákinthos and **Corfu** have a wide range of accommodation but not in high summer; many hotels are open all year round.

WHERE TO EAT

Eating places in and around the islands abound and cater for the tourist with a familiar selection of Greek specialities from starters to grills and fish. There is no shortage of tavernas and restaurants and you may peruse the menu before deciding to sit down to eat.

SHOPPING

Internationally rated designer Lisa Palavicini hails from **Corfu** and has an outlet for clothes at Panton (off Panton Street). **Lefkáda** is famed for its lace and embroidery and **Zákinthos** doess a delicious white nougat with almonds.

USEFUL CONTACTS

Tourist Police:
Corfu, tel: (0661) 30-265.
Itháki, tel: (0674) 32-205.
Kefaloniá, tel: (0671) 22-200.
Kýthira, tel: (0735) 31-206.
Lefkáda, tel: (0645) 22-346.
Paxí, tel: (0662) 31-222.
Zákinthos, tel: (0695) 27-367.

IONIAN ISLANDS	J	F	M	A	M	J	J	A	S	O	N	D
AVERAGE TEMP. °F	57	57	61	64	73	81	84	84	81	73	66	61
AVERAGE TEMP. °C	14	14	16	18	23	27	29	29	27	23	19	16
HOURS OF SUN DAILY	4	5	6	7	10	11	12	11	9	7	5	4
RAINFALL ins.	4.5	4.5	3	2.5	1	0.5	0	0.5	1.5	4	6	5
RAINFALL mm	111	113	76	62	20	13	6	9	35	105	152	127
DAYS OF RAINFALL	13	13	10	9	5	1	1	2	4	10	12	14

7
The Dodecanese

The influence of successive rulers – Venetian, Ottoman and Italian – have given the Dodecanese a distinct character and architecture. The name Dodecanese (12 islands) is a misnomer: twelve islands, and no one knows which, were mentioned in Byzantine times and the name stuck.

There are 16 'inhabited' islands and up to 27 in total – some of them bare, limestone outcrops; **Níssyros** alone is volcanic. **Rhodes** is the administrative and economic centre of the prefecture but the islands are often considered as two distinct groups: northern and southern Dodecanese, centred on Kos and Rhodes respectively.

Rhodes (Ródos) and **Kos** are among the most popular international tourist attractions in the Mediterranean with a pace of life to match. **Lipsí**, **Chálki**, and **Níssyros** offer a complete contrast, being untouched by mass tourism. **Pátmos**, dominated by its monastery, is still delightful in spite of the numbers of pilgrims. Wild, unspoiled **Kárpathos**, the second largest of the islands, has a superb coastline and is a mass of wildflowers in spring. **Sými**, having no water must restrict visitors and, like **Tílos**, has an air of exclusivity. **Léros** has suffered from the notoriety of its mental hospitals; **Kálimnos** now relies on tourism following the decline of its sponge fishing industry; **Kastellórizo** is excellent for snorkelling. Both **Kássos** and **Agathonísi** are barren, hilly and difficult to reach – definitely appealing for those who hate crowds. **Astypálaia** – in both geographical location and appearance – owes more to the Cyclades than Dodecanese.

DON'T MISS

*** Rhodes: the Inns of the Knights and the preserved Mediaeval town.
*** Rhodes: picturesque Líndos town with its ancient acropolis and the Dorian city of Kámiros.
** Kárpathos: Olympos Village – a repository of island customs and folklore.
** Kastellórizo: the blue grotto of Perásta with its illuminated stalactites.
* Pátmos: Monastery of St John the Divine who wrote his Revelations on the island.

Opposite: *Líndos, where white houses ring the acropolis, is one of the best-loved places in Greece.*

RHODES (RODOS) ***

Rhodes (area 1398km²; 540 sq miles), was claimed
by the ancients to be 'more beautiful than the sun' –
clearly, from the vast numbers of visitors, many still
think that description pertains. Today, this fertile island
is a year-round top international resort where the sun
shines for over 300 days of the year.

The tourist presence is largely concentrated in the
north of the island, especially around **Rhodes town**:
south of **Líndos** and **Péfkos** it is still possible to escape
crowds and, outside the main tourist season, find solitude.
Rhodes is an excellent base from which to begin island-
hopping and also an important point of call on
international routes to
Cyprus, Israel and Egypt.

Rhodes town presents a
particularly attractive face
to those arriving by boat at
night when the massive
city walls, minarets, **Palace
of the Grand Masters** and
windmills on the harbour
are illuminated. Rhodes,
the main port and town,
was founded in 480BC
and became an important
trading and cultural centre
in the Hellenic world.

There are seven surviv-
ing gates to **Old Rhodes
Town**, magnificent legacy
of the **Knights of St John**
who made it their own
from 1309. In summer the
old town heaves with
approximately 50,000 visitors a day: restaurants have
menus in English, German
and Swedish and prices are
inflated. The **Palace of the**

Grand Masters, damaged in an explosion in 1856, was reconstructed by the Italians in 1939 and used by Benito Mussolini (open Tuesday–Sunday 08:00–19:00, Monday 12:00–09:00). The **Street of the Knights** begins from the Platía Kleovólou in front of the palace, with eight **Inns** built for each of the nationalities within the order and today housing various government and cultural agencies. The original **Hospital of the Knights** is now the Archaeological Museum and the old **Cathedral of the Knights** across from it is the Byzantine Museum (both open Tuesday–Sunday 08:30–15:00). Within the old town there are remnants of later cultures: the **Süleyman Mosque** is still used for worship by a Muslim minority and there is a working *hammam* – Turkish bath. The old **Jewish Quarter** lies east of the Koskinoú (Ioánnis) Gate around the **Platía Evréon Martýron** (Square of the Martyrs), its fountain topped by three sea horses in bronze. The centuries old community was brutally exterminated under German occupation. Outside the walls, the new town offers all the delights (and horrors) of any cosmopolitan shopping centre.

The entrance to **Mandráki** (Limani Mandrákiou), the old harbour, is watched over by the **Platóni** – a bronze stag and doe each atop a stone pillar. A trio of windmills (late 15th century) stands on the harbour where they once milled grain for cargo ships.

Rhodes

Index		
1. Inn of Auvergne	6. Inn of France
2. Platia Simis	7. Inn of Provence
3. Inn of England	8. Inn of Spain
4. Museum of Rhodes	9. Cannon Gate
5. Inn of Italy	10. St. Mary's Tower
	11. Kastellania

Below: *Twin towers dominate the Palace of the Grand Masters.*

Monte Smith (named after an English Admiral), is the
site of Hellenistic Rhodes, 2km (1½ miles) west of the main
town. Remains are sparse – a few columns of a **Temple of
Apollo**, restored **Ancient Theatre** and **Odeon**.

The Knights once grew their medicinal herbs in **Rodíni
Park**, 2km (1½ miles) south of Rhodes on the Líndos Road.
In late August the park hosts the **Rhodes Wine Festival**
but in ancient times the park rang to different sounds, for
here Aeschines established his famous School of Rhetoric.
Distinguished alumni included Pompey, Cicero, Cassius,
Julius Caesar, Brutus and Mark Anthony.

Líndos, on the east coast, with its dazzling, white
houses on a fortress-topped hill at the end of a sweeping
bay is a marvel – not so the line of tourist coaches. Out of
season and crowd-free, the charm of the labyrinthine
streets returns. First inhabited by Minoans, a natural harbour led to Líndos becoming one of three important
cities on the island. The **acropolis** was fortified by the
Knights and now the ruins of the ancient city lie within
massive walls – reached by a climb or on donkey-back.
The **Bay of St Paul** below the acropolis is where the
apostle is said to have landed in AD58.

Eptá Pigés is an Italian-made lake fed by seven
springs. It lies 5km (3 miles) inland from crowded
Tsambíka and suffers from the inevitable tourist attention – in spring the area is
delightful with birdsong
(nightingales) and wildflowers.

The rocky coast immediately
west of Rhodes town is developed with hotels offering every
facility one could want. Above
Triánda are the remains of
ancient **Iálysos** on the slopes of
Mt Filérimos, where in spring,
the pine-covered slopes boast
superb wildflowers. There is a
reconstructed Doric fountain
(4th century BC) and remains of
a **Temple of Athena Polias**

Below: Every turn in
old Rhodes town brings
the fascination of old houses,
arches and churches.

Left: *Tsambíka is one of the best beaches on Rhodes, but very crowded in season.*

THE KNIGHTS OF ST JOHN

Following the fall of Jerusalem in1291 the Knights Hospitallers of St John were expelled. They took up residence at Kolossi in Cyprus and dedicated themselves to protecting pilgrims and tending to the sick through their herbal remedies (and some claim 'magical arts'). They set their sights on Rhodes and by 1309 had secured their aims. Later, they became an irritant to the Ottoman forces and in 1522 Süleyman the Magnificent sent 100,000 of his troops against them. After a long battle the Knights were defeated, and allowed to leave for Malta where the order lived until 1798 when Napoleon annexed the island.

and **Zeus Polieus**. Pride of place goes to the **Monastery of Our Lady of Filérimos** with its domed chapels, converted by the Knights from an early basilica.

Ancient **Kámiros** is superbly sited on a terraced hill above the sea. Here are the remains of a Dorian city which, with Líndos and Iálysos, united to found the city of Rhodes in 408BC. **Kámiros Skála**, with its sleepy harbour, lies 16km (10 miles) south of Kámiros: from here boats run to **Chálki**. The **Kastéllos** (one of the Knights' ruins) sits high above steep cliffs where ravens, crag martins and blue rock thrush make their homes.

A car is a necessity for exploring the interior of the island: there is a leisurely route by road around **Mt Profítis Ilías** (800m; 2625ft) and paths lead into the extensive pine forest where the native white peonies (*Paeonia rhodia*) flower in spring. Walkers can find more of a challenge on **Mt Atáviros** (1215m; 3986ft) by undertaking the six hour walk over the summit from**Embónas** to **Agios Isídoros**.

Monólithos village in the far south, where the mountains of the interior reach the sea, sits as an isolated hill topped by a ruined Crusader castle. The setting is superb, offering breathtaking views and, like **Kataviá** and the lovely beaches of **Cape Prasoníssi** at the southern tip, a million miles from the bustle of the city.

LINDOS' BEACHES

Although Líndos beach is crowded, the bays south of **Lardhós** are less frequented. The coast north of Líndos offers a number of good but busy beaches from **Kalithéa** to **Faliráki** – the island's major resort featuring every watersport imaginable for the 18–30 set. **Afándou** is slightly quieter and has an 18-hole golf course; south of **Kolímbia** the beaches near **Vágia point** are still unspoiled.

Above: *Pothiá, capital of Kálimnos, is a surprisingly large town with traditional Greek cafés and restaurants.*
Opposite: *Ladies of Olympos in traditional dress keep alive the 'old ways' of island life.*

VALLEY OF THE BUTTERFLIES

Petaloúdhes, the 'Valley of the Butterflies' on Rhodes, is a summer attraction where **Jersey tiger moths** (*Euplagia quadripunctaria*) – not butterflies – gather in their thousands in the cool, damp valley. Visitors are warned not to disturb the creatures as their numbers decrease annually but some people are tempted to put them to flight (the flash of bright orange under wings is spectacular). The valley is well-signposted west of Marítsa, off the road from Psinthós to Kalamón. In recent years fires have damaged the woods.

ASTYPÁLAIA ★

Although regarded as the most westerly member of the Dodecanese, Astypálaia owes much to the neighbouring eastern Cyclades, both in its barren landscape and clean white 'cubist' houses. **Chóra**, the upper town, is a maze of narrow lanes developed from a 9th-century-fortification which was rebuilt by Venetians on the site of the ancient acropolis. The climb from the harbour offers spectacular views and a line of nine ruined windmills. Reliable bus services provide connections with **Livádia** in a lush valley leading to a good shingle beach and with **Maltezána**, once a pirate lair. **Vathí**, the island's second port, lies in an inlet which forms a deep natural harbour.

CHÁLKI ★

Copper ore was once mined on the island, hence the origin of its name. The island (area 28km²; 11 sq miles) is a dry rock, unspoiled and good for walking. **Emborió** has impressive Venetian-style houses, a row of ruined windmills and the **Church of Agios Nikólaos** boasting the tallest campanile in the Dodecanese. **Chorió**, the island's other village, is overlooked by a ruined castle. There are boat trips around the island and to abandoned **Alimnía**, a green islet with wonderful beaches and a crusader castle.

KÁLIMNOS ★★

This scenically dramatic island (area 111 km²; 43 sq miles) is completely unspoiled and rises to 700m (2300ft) at **Profítis Ilías** in its centre. Kálimnos still maintains a thriving sponge diving trade although many people have had to leave the island for economic reasons. The main tourist development stretches between **Massoúri** and **Myrtiés** on the west coast. Islanders claim that the sunsets over **Telendos** islet are the finest in all Greece.

Volcanic activity shaped the valley of **Váthi** and left it
with the fertile soils now used for growing citrus – it runs
to the sea at **Rína** and forms a deep inlet. A boat is needed
to reach **Daskaleío**, a cave at the mouth of the inlet which
has yielded finds from Neolithic and Bronze ages.

PSERIMOS *

A favourite with day trippers from **Kos** and **Kálimnos**
who throng to its sandy beach. Accommodation is limited
as fewer than a hundred people live here but the island is
completely different after the sightseers have gone.

KÁRPATHOS ***

Kárpathos with its wild, rugged landscape is still quiet
and unspoiled, even though it boasts a new international
airport. With two craggy mountains rising to over
1000m (3281ft) and superb wildflowers, it is a paradise
for walkers and naturalists: the extensive beaches with
white sands are often empty.

Many people visit Kárpathos just to see the village of
Olympos high in its mountain stronghold and reached
by minibus from the harbour at **Diafáni**. It is a popular
tourist destination but remains a treasure house of old
buildings with decorated balconies, aged windmills and
traditional customs.

Although a track leads southwards from Olympos to
Spoa it can only be traversed by four-wheel-drive vehicle
or on foot so most visitors use a caique from **Diafáni** to
Pigadia, the island capital. This is
an uncompromisingly Greek town
situated in **Vróntis Bay**, with a
sandy beach north of the town.
The island's main tourist resort is
at **Ammopí**, around the headland.

Regular caiques leave Pigádia
for the superb beaches of **Kyrá
Panayía** and **Apélla** at the foot
of dramatic **Mt Kalilimni** (1188m;
3898ft), the highest mountain in
the Dodecanese.

On the west coast, **Arkássa** is rapidly becoming a holiday resort. Caiques travel to the island of Kássos from **Finíki**, a pretty fishing village with a sandy beach.

A narrow road encircles Mt Profítis Ilías, west of Pigadia. **Apéri**, the last village before the road returns to Pigadia, was once the capital and has the reputation of being one of Greece's richest villages. Many expatriates have also built houses there.

From **Diafáni** there are Sunday boat trips to the islet of **Sariá** which forms the northern tip to Kárpathos.

KÁSSOS *

Remote from everywhere, Kássos is a depopulated, almost treeless island (area 66km²; 25 sq miles) with a wild coast and several sea grottoes. The island was the first stop on Ibrahim Pasha's foray to put down the Greek rebellion against Turkish Occupation in 1824. The island's men were slaughtered and women and children enslaved. The island's few villages, mainly concentrated in the north, are untouched by tourism and visitors have to transfer via caique when seas are rough.

Fri, a fishing village, is the island's capital; **Agia Marína** has an airstrip and beach (**Ammoua**). The main attraction for visitors is the the stalactite-filled cave of **Hellenokamára**, a shrine since Mycenaean times. The best beaches are at **Chelanthrós Bay**, a walk through citrus groves from **Arvanitochóri**, and on **Armathía**, a rocky islet just off the coast.

KASTELLÓRIZO (MEGISTI) *

Mégisti's one town is full of ruined houses, some of which are being restored. The fort on the harbour was built by the **Knights of St John** but earlier inhabitants left a Lycian tomb and Doric fortress at **Palaeokástro**. There are no beaches but the blue grotto at Perásta is well known: the stalactite colours are best seen during early morning when sun light filters in.

Below: *Kastellórizo with its numerous islets forms Greece's easternmost point.*

Kos ★★★

Its central position on ferry routes makes Kos an excellent starting point for island hopping – additionally, numerous smaller boats connect Kos with the islands. Kos is replete with fast food joints and gift shops but in spite of mass tourism much of the charm of Kos town has survived. The **Defterdar Mosque** (still used) dominates **Platía Eleftherías** where you will also find the **Museum** (open Tuesday–Sunday 08:00–14:30) with its statue of Hippocrates (4th century BC), fruit market and **Pórta tou Foroú** (gate to the ancient **Agora**). The **Mosque of the Loggia** was built to overlook Hippocrates'

ancient plane tree with its huge trunk. The **Castle of the Knights of St John** was built using stones from the Agora. Along Grigoriou Street lies a **Roman Odeon** with marbled seats and nearby a gymnasium, Christian basilica and font from the 5th century have been uncovered.

The **Asklepeíon** in the hills southwest of Kos town was built after the death of Hippocrates. The ruins visible today date from the Hellenistic period.

Inland lie **Agios Pávlos** and **Agios Ioánnis** – two ruined Byzantine basilicas near **Zipári** on the road to **Asfendíou** set in pine woods country. From here a road leads to dramatic **Palaío Pili**, a deserted Byzantine town perched on a crag. **Ziá**, a popular 'tourist village', is also a base for the ascent of **Mt Orómedon** or **Díkaios Christos** (685m; 2248ft), the highest mountain on Kos.

BEACHES ON KOS

Psalídi and **Agios Fokás** are heavily developed. **Embrós Thermá** has black sands, thermal springs and fewer visitors. **Kardaména** and **Mastichári** have good beaches but are crowded in season. The coast between **Kamári** and **Agios Stéfanos** is dominated by a Club Med complex; both **Camel** and **Paradise** beaches are superb. The ruins of a 5th-century basilica of Agios Stéfanos with mosaics and columns stand near **Kamári** beach.

Above: *Two-wheeled transport is an aid to the ministry of at least one priest on Léros.*

LÉROS *

Léros has never touted its charms to tourists as it is home to three of Greece's mental hospitals and has not seemed like the obvious holiday destination. In 1989 there was an international outcry at conditions in the mental hospitals. This publicity served to focus tourist attention on a beautiful island worth visiting and Léros has since become very popular.

The port of **Lakki**, set in an inlet, is full of art-deco buildings – above it a road climbs to **Plátanos** with a Byzantine Kástro and then down to **Agia Marína** (the old port) on the east coast. **Pantéli**, southeast of **Plátanos**, has a small fishing harbour and sandy beach where the fish restaurants are very good.

LIPSÍ **

Mythology recounts that Odysseus was held on Lipsí for seven years under the spell of sea nymph Calypso and the charm of this island gem has not dulled. The island is the largest in an archipelago of tiny islets (area 16km²; 6 sq miles): most visitors are day-trippers from Léros and Pátmos attracted by its superb beaches. **Lendoú**, the town beach, is popular, **Platís Gialós** the favourite. Local wines and cheeses made from sheep and goat milk are excellent.

NÍSSYROS *

A favourite day trip from Kos is to Níssyros, a surprisingly lush volcanic island. Many beaches have black rocks and grey sands although at **Lies** they are bronze and at **Pachia Ammos** reddish; white sands occur on the islets of **Yiali** and **Agios Antonis**. Most life centres around **Mandráki**: above the town is the **Kástro** with a castle built by the Knights of St John and within it is **Panayia Spilianí**, the church of the **Madonna of the Cave**. Higher up lies the **Doric Paliokástro** with vast rock walls. **At Loutrá** there are hot springs from the volcano and **Nikiá** has a caldera where the air is pungent with sulphur and the vista is a moonscape of greys and yellows.

NEIGHBOURS

Boats leave **Pátmos** for:
• **Agathónissi:** a hilly, scrub-covered island. The small community is devoted to fishing and there are six sparsely inhabited islets nearby, including Arkí and Maráthi.
• **Arkí:** a small island of scrub-covered dunes and about 50 inhabitants. Boats from Arkí come out optimistically to meet the caiques.
• **Maráthi:** with its beach and seasonal tavernas, it's the main destination. The taverna, like that on Arkí, offer rooms for rent during the summer.

PÁTMOS *

Pátmos is a place of pilgrimage for Christians the world over drawn by the **Monastery of St John the Theologian** with its magnificent frescoes and icons.

Boats put into the harbour at **Skala** and it is a short walk to **Chóra** and the monastery. Below the monastery is the cave wherein St John is said to have had the visions which resulted in the **Book of Revelations**. The coastline hides a wealth of small bays and pebble beaches – caiques operate a water taxi service to **Lámbi** and **Psilí Ammos**, north and south of the island respectively.

SÝMI **

In ancient times **Sými** grew rich on the profits from sponge fishing and boat building and in Greek mythology its shipwrights built the *Argo* for Jason.

Illuminated tiers of house above the port at **Yialós** make it appealing by night but during the day large numbers of daytrippers from Rhodes make escape attractive – to the castle or to beaches such as Pédi or by caique to **Agios Nikólaos** or **Marathoúnda**. The **Monastery of Taxiárchis Michael Panormítis** (patron saint of sailors) is popular with sightseers. **Sesklí**, the islet off the southern tip, provides the monks with produce.

TÍLOS **

Tílos was known in antiquity for manufacture of perfume. The Knights of St John took over its administration in 1309 and built seven fortresses across the island as part of their outer defences of Rhodes.

The capital **Megálo Chorió** is a delightful whitewashed village with a Venetian Kástro and church dedicated to the Archangel Michael. **Livádia**, the port, is the only other inhabited village. One of the best walks leads above the west coast to the Byzantine **Monastery of Agios Panteleímon**.

FOSSILS FOUND

Bones of deer, tortoises and dwarf elephant (*mastodon*) only 1.3m (4ft) tall ,were found in 1971 in a ravine near the deserted village of **Mikró Chorío**. The island is believed to have been joined to Asia Minor until the Pleistocene period (time of the last ice age in Europe). More recent remains were revealed at **Agios Antónis** where there is a row of human skeletons on the beach thought to belong to villagers caught in lava in 600BC when Níssyros erupted.

Below: *Sými's tiered port is a favourite with daytrippers from Rhodes.*

The Dodecanese at a Glance

Mild weather and lack of crowds make Kos and Rhodes excellent **winter** destinations – smaller islands virtually close down. **Spring** begins in late February and flowers are superb on both Rhodes and Kárpathos, particularly **March–April**. **May** is excellent for walking. Summer visitors increase from **June** and most accommodation is pre-booked. By **October** crowds have gone but the sea is still warm and swimming is great.

In summer numerous **direct charters** operate to Rhodes and Kos from major European destinations; charter flights to Kárpathos depart from the UK. Other flights to and between islands are operated by Olympic Airways.
Scheduled Olympic Flights: **Astypálaia** Athens (2 weekly). **Kos** Athens (3 daily), Rhodes (3 weekly). Olympic, tel: (0242) 28-331.
Kássos Rhodes (daily), Kárpathos and Sitía in Crete (2–3 weekly). Olympic, tel: (0254) 41-555.
Kárpathos Athens (2-3 weekly) Rhodes (2–7 daily), Kássos and Sitía (2–3 weekly), tel: (0245) 22-150.
Kastellórizo Rhodes (2–3 weekly). Olympic, tel: (0241) 49-241.
Léros Athens (daily). Olympic, tel: (0247) 22-844.
Rhodes Athens (4 daily) plus

connections with Crete (Iráklion), Thessaloníki, Rome, Kárpathos, Kássos, Kos, Thíra, Kastellórizo, Mýkonos. Domestic flights from Olympic, tel: (0241) 24-555. Up to 10 large **ferries** per week make the Piraeus to Rhodes (18–20 hours) trip either travelling direct (with an extension to Cyprus – Limassol on some routes) or via other islands in the group.**Piraeus**, **Pátmos**, **Léros**, **Kálimnos**, **Kos**, **Rhodes**. In summer the route is extended on weekends to **Crete (Iráklion)** via Chálki, Kássos and Kárpathos.**Rhodes** is a good centre for reaching smaller islands in the **Dodecanese**: 1 weekly to Tílos, Níssyros, Astypálaia, Kos, Kálimnos, Chálki and also to Kárpathos. Rhodes to **Cyclades**: 2–3 weekly to Thíra, Páros, Mýkonos, Tínos, Andros and Rafína (mainland). Rhodes to **Aegean Islands**: 1 weekly to Folégandros, Mílos, Sífnos, Ikaría, Sámos, Chíos and Lésbos. **Hydrofoils** operate daily services to Kos, Pátmos and Sými with connections to Kálimnos, Léros, Níssyros, Tílos and also Chálki.
International ferry routes link Rhodes with Italy (Venice), Cyprus (Limassol), Egypt (Alexandria), Israel (Haifa) and Turkey (Bodrum).
For **island hoppers** the *Níssos Kálymnos* car ferry visits each island of the Dodecanese at least once a week between March and December.

Schedules vary and boats are often late so get details from its base on Kálimnos, tel: (0243) 29-612.
Agathóníssi ferries also 2 weekly with Arki, Lipsi, Pátmos,Sámos and Chíos.
Hydrofoil 1 weekly to Kos, Kálimnos, Léros, Pátmos and Sámos (Pithagório).
Arkí occasional caiques from Pátmos, Maráthi (*see* also Agathóníssi).
Astypálaia ferries 3 weekly with Sýros, Rhodes, Tílos and Níssyros, 3 weekly with Kos, Kálimnos, Amorgós, Mýkonos, Tínos and Piraeus, 1 weekly to Páros and Náxos. Once a week in summer to Thíra, Andros, and Rafína. **Port Authority**, tel: (0243) 61-208.
Chálki daily links with Rhodes (Kámiros Skála) plus occasional hydrofoils. Once a week with Kárpathos, Kássos, Sitía (Crete), Sými, Thíra, Síkinos, Folégandros, Mílos, Sífnos, Piraeus. **Port Authority**, tel: (0241) 45-220.
Kálimnos daily ferries to Piraeus, Rhodes, Kos, Léros and Pátmos, 4 weekly to Sámos, 3 weekly to Lipsí and Astypálaia. 1 weekly to Lésbos, Límnos, Ikaría, Mýkonos, Thíra, Tínos, Andros, Rafína and Thessaloníki – (*see* also island Hoppers). **Port Authority**, tel: (0243) 29-304.
Kárpathos ferries to Piraeus (3 weekly) and Rhodes (4 weekly), also 3 weekly with Thíra; 2 weekly with Kássos, Mílos and Crete, 1 weekly with Páros,

The Dodecanese at a Glance

Síkinos, Folégandros and Sífnos. **Port Authority**, tel: (0245) 22-227.

Kássos 2 weekly with Piraeus, Crete, Kárpathos, Mílos and Rhodes, 1 weekly with Chálki, Sými, Thíra, Síkinos, Sífnos and Folégandros. **Port Authority**, tel: (0254) 41-288.

Kastellórizo (Mégisti) 1–2 weekly from Rhodes. **Port Authority**, tel: (0241) 49-270.

Kos daily to Piraeus, Rhodes, Kálimnos, Léros and Pátmos, 3 weekly to Tílos, Mýkonos, Andros, and Rafína, 2 weekly to Sámos, Sými, Kastellórizo and Astypálaia. **Hydrofoils** provide daily links with Sámos and Rhodes and several go weekly to Kálimnos, Léros, Lipsí, Pátmos, Ikaría, Sými, Níssyros plus one per week to Agathonísi. **Port Authority**, tel: (0242) 26-594.

Léros daily except Sunday with Piraeus, Pátmos; 9 times a week to Kálimnos; Kos, 5 weekly to Rhodes; 1 per week to Sámos, Ikaría, Chíos, Lésbos, Límnos and Kavála. Hydrofoils daily from Agia Marína to Kálimnos, Kos, Pátmos and Sámos. **Port Authority**, tel: (0247) 22-224.

Lipsí ferries 3 weekly with Sámos, Pátmos, Léros and Kálimnos, 2 weekly to Kos and Agathonísi, 1 weekly to Níssyros, Tílos, Sými, Ikaría and Rhodes. Daily excursions to Léros (Agia Marína) and Pátmos (Skála) make links with overnight-ferries calling at Pátmos. **Port Authority**,

tel: (0247) 41-240.

Níssyros and **Pserimos** daily excursions from Kos. **Port Authority**, tel: (0242) 32-222.

Pátmos daily ferries to Piraeus link with others on Dodecanese route (Pátmos, Léros, Kálimnos, Kos, Rhodes). 4 weekly to Sámos, 3 weekly to Ikaría, 2 weekly Agathonísi, 1 weekly to Sámos, Chíos, Lésbos, Límnos and Kavala. Hydrofoil services in summer run to Léros, Kálimnos, Kos, Agathonísi, and Sámos (Pithagorio) plus a service to Sámos (Váthi and Karlóvasi) via Ikaría and beyond to Chíos and Lésbos. **Port Authority**, tel: (0247) 34-131.

Sými daily ferries to and from Rhodes; tourist boats in season. 2–3 weekly to Piraeus via Tílos, Níssyros Kos, Léros, Kálimnos, Lipsí, Pátmos, Náxos. **Port Authority**, tel: (0241) 71-205.

GETTING AROUND

On **Kos** and **Rhodes** reliable bus services connect main towns and resorts. On smaller islands such as **Astypálaia and Kálimnos** there are regular bus services. On most islands larger villages are linked by one bus per day which leaves

early and returns at night. Shared taxis are a way of life for most islanders. In season boats and sometimes hydrofoils provide the easiest links between main coastal towns and beaches. (see page 124 for on-line timetable and bookings.

WHERE TO STAY

(see At a Glance p. 113).

WHERE TO EAT

(see At a Glance p. 113).

TOURS AND EXCURSIONS

Coach trips offered on Rhodes and Kos: travel agents and hotels carry details.

USEFUL CONTACTS

Tourist Police:
Astypálaia, tel: (0242) 61-207.
Kálimnos, tel: (0243) 29-301.
Kárpathos, tel: (0245) 22-222.
Kássos, tel: (0254) 41-222.
Kastellórizo, tel: (0241) 29-068.
Kos, tel: (0242) 22-444.
Léros, tel: (0247) 22-222.
Lipsí, tel: (0247) 41-222.
Níssyros, tel: (0242) 31-201.
Pátmos, tel: (0247) 31-303.
Rhodes, tel: (0241) 27-423
Sými, tel: (0241) 71-238.
Tílos, tel: (0241) 44-222.

DODECANESE	J	F	M	A	M	J	J	A	S	O	N	D
AVERAGE TEMP. °F	52	54	57	61	68	75	79	79	73	68	61	55
AVERAGE TEMP. °C	11	12	14	16	20	24	26	26	23	20	16	13
HOURS OF SUN DAILY	5	5	6	7	10	11	12	11	9	7	5	4
RAINFALL ins.	4.5	3	3	2	1	0.5	0	0	0.5	3	3	4.5
RAINFALL mm	114	73	70	43	18	8	1	0	13	73	82	110
DAYS OF RAINFALL	9	9	8	7	6	3	1	2	2	6	9	9

8
The Northeastern Aegean

If anything links the seven major islands and four islets of the northeastern Aegean Isles it is their individuality. In the north, **Thásos** is a popular tourist destination enveloped by lovely sandy beaches and wooded hills, **Samothráki** (Samothrace) is craggy with dramatic seascapes and **Límnos** has a delightful port town.

Lésbos, **Chíos** and **Sámos** figured prominently in ancient Greece as 'stepping stones' to Asia Minor. They were also famed for their sailors, the excellence of their arts, sciences and luminaries such as **Homer** (Chíos), **Pythagoras** (Sámos) and **Sappho** (Lésbos). Today, they might be a short distance physically from **Turkey** but politically lie as far removed as ever. Few signs of their Ottoman heritage remain and a strong Greek military presence is maintained. Day trips to Turkey are possible from the islands – the fare is nothing short of exploitative.

Lésbos, third largest island in Greece, is embraced by the 'up-market' package trade while verdant, forested **Sámos** (with frequent caique connections to popular **Pátmos**) is almost part of the Dodecanese. West of Sámos, precipitous **Ikaría**, with its thermal springs, is still relatively unspoiled and nearby **Foúrni** is a definite 'away-from-it-all' island. **Agios Efstrátios**, south of Límnos, was decimated by an earthquake in 1968 and has never really recovered – everything, water included, is imported.

Chíos is suddenly being discovered by the more discerning tourist wanting something definitely Greek: local ferries connect with **Psará** and **Inoússes**, both islets with permanent populations of only a few hundred.

●ATHENS

DON'T MISS

*** Chíos: unique Pirgí and the houses of the other mastic villages with their lovely geometric painted walls.
*** Sámos: Pithagória with its huge archaeological site; temples and the amazing Efplinion Tunnel.
** Lésbos: mediaeval hill village of Agiássos and Mt Olympos – mountain walks with spectacular views.
* Thásos: an island ringed with lovely beaches.

Opposite: *The geometri-cally decorated houses of Pirgí, one of the mastic villages on Chíos.*

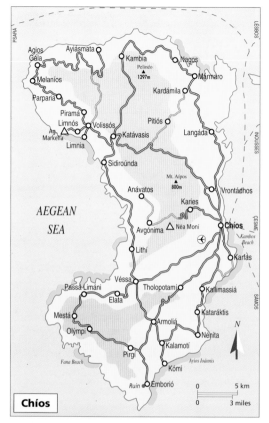

Chíos

CHÍOS (HIOS) ★★★

Many Chíots have a polite, natural reserve which some mistake for unfriendliness. Chíos is a land of contrasts – fertile plains, verdant valleys, pine forests and barren mountains. The island is 852km² (329 sq miles).

At first sight **Chíos town** (Chóra) seems to be a busy commercial centre with an unprepossessing industrial waterfront. But a little exploration pays dividends. Within the Byzantine fortress there is a ruined mosque and Ottoman houses with latticed windows and balconies. **Kastro Justinian Museum** has an intriguing collection of frescoes, mosaics and carvings (open Tuesday–Sunday 09:00–15:00). In nearby Platía Vournakíou is the **Byzantine Museum** housed in an old mosque (open daily 10:00–13:00; Sunday 10:00–15:00). Near the cathedral is the large **Koraï Municipal Library** (open Monday–Saturday 08:00–14:00) established in 1792 and, within the same building, the **Argenti Folklore Museum** with a fascinating collection of village costumes and artefacts.

The **Kámbos** is a vast, fertile plain south of Chóra with a maze of lanes. Here the Genoese built their mansions amidst fertile gardens of citrus and mulberry trees. The old stone water wheels (*manganós*) and wooden bridges can be discovered on foot or by bicycle.

Inland from Chíos town, the first monastery of **Néa Moní** was built where a miraculous icon of the Virgin appeared: its replacement was built in 1042 by the Emperor Constantine VIII Monomachos. The 11th-century mosaics are superb – they were reassembled in 1881 after an earthquake collapsed the dome. From **Avgónima** a road climbs to the deserted mediaeval village of **Anátavos**. It is reputedly haunted by ghosts of desperate villagers who threw themselves from the cliffs rather than suffer at the hands of the Turks in 1822.

· Centuries of shipbuilding and recent fires have destroyed most of the northern forests. Wealthy **Vrontádhos** with its ruined windmills is the home of shipowning families and site of the **Dhaskalópetra** (teacher's rock) where the poet Homer is said to have taught and performed his works. Inland and usually reached by taxi is the village of **Pitiós**, said to be the birthplace of Homer.

One of the island's best beaches lies at **Skála Volissoú** (Limiá), just below **Volissós**, where caiques leave for the island of **Psará**. More beaches are to be found at **Chóri** (a nudist beach), and **Limnós**. To the southeast near **Katávasis**, dramatically set in barren mountains lies **Moní Moúdon** (a 13th-century monastery); to the north is **Piramá** with the delightful **Church of Agios Ioánnis**, known for its icons and a mediaeval tower.

Above: *Néa Moní, home of a revered icon.*
Below: *the decorated tradition (*xistá*) of the mastic villages was taught to the locals by the Genoese.*

Above: *Anaxos village lies on a sweeping bay – peace and quiet a short distance from Mólyvos at the northern tip.*

LÉSBOS (MITILINI) **

Although Lésbos is the third largest island in Greece (1630km²; 629 sq miles), many of its villages preserve a traditional way of life – from their balconied houses to music and customs. Lésbos is a well forested island: in spite of severe fires an estimated 13 million olive trees grow here. Naturalists favour Lésbos because of its rare flowers and migrating birds, and from antiquity to the present visitors have enjoyed the island as a centre for creative and performing arts.

Venerable mansions, imposing public buildings and plentiful municipal gardens are features of **Mitilíni**; a **Byzantine kástro**, later fortified by the Genoese, stands on a peninsula in the bay. West of the city are traces of its Classical past: here stood one of the largest **Hellenistic theatres** in Greece and nearby are remains of a **Roman aqueduct** and part of the ancient city walls. The **Archaeology Museum** (open Tuesday–Sunday 08:00–14:30) has Roman reliefs and Greek mosaics. The **Museum of Traditonal Arts and Crafts** (hours variable) documents island life in the villages, while the small **Byzantine Museum** (open Monday–Saturday 09:00–13:00) is part of a church, **Agios Therápon**, built on the site of a Christian basilica.

Loutrá Géras, one of the island's five excellent spas, lies to the south of Mitilíni and is easily reached by bus (*see* page 113).

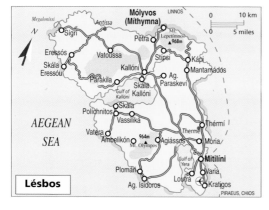

Lésbos

Mt Olympos (964m; 3162ft) with its extensive pine and chestnut woodlands lies east of Mytilíni and dominates the south of the island. On its eastern face **Agiássos**, a large mediaeval hill village, has become a tourist attraction with its castle, red-roofed houses, traditional vases, walnuts and plums. There is a lengthy but superb walk down to the coast at **Plomári** via **Palaiókastro** and **Melaglochóri**. At **Vaterá** graceful sea daffodils flower in summer on the long beach and there is a collection of remarkable fossils at **Vrissa** (*see* page 113).

Near **Mória** to the north of **Mitilíni** are intact arches of a Roman aqueduct – the road carries on to **Thermí** where the hot mineral springs were used by Romans and much earlier civilizations. From **Mantamádos** (famous for its *koumária* – earthenware jugs) the road turns inland towards the church **Taxiarchis Michael** which has a miraculous black icon. The scenery around **Mt Lepetímnos** (968m; 3176ft) is dramatic and wild and hiking trails have been laid out to meet the needs of increasing numbers of walkers.

Local buses travelling across country take the inland road northwest of **Mitilíni** to **Kallóni** where the medieval Kástro was constructed on the site of ancient **Arisbe**. A road runs via **Keramía** down to **Skála Kallóni** on Kalloní bay. The bay is almost a lagoon and numerous water birds are attracted to a series of saltpans: there are black-winged stilts, avocets and both black and white storks. In spring the reed beds are alive with frogs, toads and pond tortoises.

Mólyvos (Míthymna) at the northern tip of the island is a striking coastal town with buildings of dark volcanic stone brightened by painted shutters, doors and windows.

The northwest of Lésbos is volcanic and yellow rhododendrons line rocky gullies in spring. Between **Eressós** and **Sígri** (and on Sarakína and Nisiópi) are remains of a forest – trunks of sequoias become visible as the sea erodes the volcanic ash which covered them.

CRADLE OF POETS

Sappho, a well-educated lady of aristocratic birth who was born in Eressós (Lésbos) around 600BC, was dubbed the 'Tenth Muse' by Plato because she was similar to the nine goddesses or muses, each of whom was regarded as a protectress of a different art or science. Her often erotic works were directed at the women of her academy – all followers of **Aphrodite**. Being too clever by half for the politicians she was perceived as a threat and her work burned. Later poets include **Alcaeus** (lyric poet), **Longus** (Daphnis and Chloë) and the modern Nobel Laureate, **Odysséas Elytis**.

Below: *The donkey is still the traditional beast of burden used to carry the fruit and olive harvests.*

Sámos

SÁMOS ★★★

This fertile 472km^2 (182 sq miles) island has always held a special place in Greek affections for its Samian wines, its boat-building and the skills of its sailors. Extensive pine forests (damaged by fire in recent years), olive groves, two substantial mountains – **Mt Ampelos** (1140m; 3740ft) and **Mt Kérkis** (1445m; 4741ft) – and a coast indented with numerous small bays contribute to the appeal of a very popular island.

Most tourism is concentrated away from the capital **Vathí** (Sámos town), an elegant, rather up-market town. The **Archaeological Museum** (open Tuesday–Sunday 08:00–14:30, *see* page 113) is outstanding with finds from Pithagório and the nearby Temple of Hera. East of Vathí, on cliffs above the fishing village of **Mourtiá** stands the **Monastery of Zoodóchos Pigí** – from here on clear days Turkey seems almost close enough to touch. To Vathí's west is **Kokkári** with whitewashed houses spread over twin headlands, and beaches at **Lemonákia** and **Tsamadoú**. **Avlákia** further west is a quiet resort and the perfect base for walking on **Mt Ampelos**.

Right: *Close to the shore at Pithagório stands a castle, built by Logothétis, a hero of the 19th-century revolution against Turkish rule.*

Pithagório, named after its favourite son, was once the islands's capital and is today the biggest tourist resort. Excavations begun in 1985 have uncovered vast lengths of walls plus traces of a theatre, Roman baths and the remarkable Efplinion Tunnel (open Monday, Thursday, Saturday 10:00–12:00) that carried water to the city. Visitors can walk the first 300m (984ft) of its 1km (½ mile) length. From the theatre a road leads to the Sybil's cave which shelters the **Church of Panayía Spilianí** carved into the rock. The **Temple of Hera** (open Tuesday–Sunday 08:00–14:30) was the third largest temple built in ancient Greece and one of the seven wonders of the ancient world. Two centuries of earthquakes and attacks by invaders eventually brought down its 133 columns and locals took stones for their buildings.

Above: *Fertile Sámos seems more lush than other Aegean Islands and the land is filled with olives, Cypress trees and pines.*

Picturesque **Limáni** – the old part of **Karlóvassi** (the island's second port) is a good base from which to explore the west of the island with its ravines and idyllic beaches such as those at **Mikró Seitáni** and **Megálo Seitáni**. The island's oldest church is the 10th-century **Panayía tou Potamoú** (Our Lady of the River) from where a track leads upstream through a gorge – to negotiate it you have to wade or swim through deep pools.

Mt Kérkis (1445m; 4741ft), a dormant volcano, dominates western Samos. A road climbs the mountain through chestnut woods as far as **Kastánea** and a track leads to the summit. On the other side of the mountain's bulk lies the resort of **Marathókampos** (with restored village houses for rent) and on the coast is the small port of **Ormós Marathokámpou** from which caiques run to the islet of **Samopoúla** in summer. Local beaches are excellent – **Votsalákia** has white sands and a path leading back up to **Mt Kérkis**, while **Psilí Ámmos** offers shallow seas.

> **THE OLDEST INHABITANTS**
>
> North of Pithagório traces of much earlier inhabitants have been found – the animals (miniature ancestors of rhinoceros, hippopotamos and horse) which roamed the island when it was apparently joined to Turkey. Their fossils, dating back 15 million years, were washed into a gorge and are now displayed in Greece's **Palaeontological Museum** in Mitilini town hall (open weekdays 09:00 –12.00; 17:00–20:00).

Agios Efstrátios *

The long name of this tiny, sunbaked, volcanic island southwest of Límnos comes from a saint who lived and died here in exile. Almost a mountain top in the sea, Agios Efstrátios (area 43km²; 17 sq miles) is well off the tourist track and as the port is too shallow for big boats, ferries are met by blue and white taxi boats.

Above: *With limited development of tourism, quiet places are easy to find in Ikarían villages.*

Ikaría **

The mountainous spine of **Mt Atheras** runs the length of Ikaría, an island long known for the curative properties of its thermal springs.

Agios Kírikos is more like a series of villages than port and capital. The spa at **Thérma**, a favourite with elderly Greeks, is more radioactive than any other in Europe. **Evdilos**, the island's second port, is connected with Agios Kiríkos by a mountain road which hangs on a cliffside for part of its length. Tourist development has centred on **Armenistís** which has a good beach, as has **Nás** just down the coast, site of an old city. Inland lies the attractive mountain village of **Christós Rachés** with its orchards and vineyards. **Manganítis**, the westernmost village, far from everywhere, has a remarkable lively atmosphere.

DAEDALUS AND IKARUS

Daedalus was the ingenious inventor and engineer who designed the labyrinth for King Minos of Crete. Unwisely, Daedalus aided the king's daughter Ariadne in saving Theseus. Minos ordered his men to watch all ports and so, in order to escape, Daedalus constructed wings for himself and his son Ikarus using feathers and wax. They flew from Crete but Ikarus flew too close to the sun, the wax melted and he plunged into the sea. The island of Ikaría rose where he fell.

Inoússes *

An archipelago of nine small islands sits in the sea east of Chíos: only the largest, Inoússes (the name means 'wine islands'), area 16km² (6 sq miles), is inhabited. The landscape is unspoiled and the few small beaches deserted. Per-capita the island is the richest in Greece being home to some 60 ship-owning families.

Most visitors come on daytrips from **Chíos** – the boats also call en route at **Mandráki**, an islet with a church.

LÍMNOS *

But for the few hills around **Mírina**, the main town, Límnos (area 477km²; 173 sq miles) is flat with endless fields of wheat, tobacco and cotton guarded by bizarre scarecrows. Mírina's main attraction is its superb **kástro** (castle) atop a rocky promontory in the middle of the bay. The **Archaeological Museum** has impressive collections taken from around the

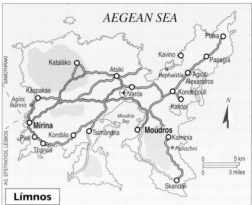

island (open Tuesday–Sunday 08:00–14:00). At **Aktí Mírina** there is a fine town beach where the Amazons of Límnos reputedly slit the throats of their husbands and threw them into the sea. There are safe pebble beaches to the north (**Agios Ioánnis** and **Avlónas**) and lovely sandy shores to the south (**Platí** and **Thános**). **Nevgátis** is generally acknowledged to be the island's best beach and nearby **Kontiás** its liveliest village – possibly something to do with the highly-rated oúzo produced there.

The east coast has the best of the archaeological sites, including **Kotsiónos** – the walled Mediaeval capital – and **Hephaistía**, still mostly unexcavated.

EVANGELISMOS

The convent of Evangelismós on Inoússes was built in the 1960s in memory of Iríni, 20-year-old daughter of Katíngo Patéras, of a prominent ship-owning family. The girl died from Hodgkinson's disease after praying to take the illness from her father who was suffering from it. After three years when her body was exhumed (local custom) it was found to be mummi-fied, convincing her mother that she was a saint.

Left: *A spectacular view of Mírina, port and capital of Límnos. Often called Kástro for its castle built over the promontory in the midst of the sandy shore.*

Below: *Doric columns re-erected at the Sanctuary of the Gods at Samothráki which marks the Hieron where final stages of initiation took place.*

SAMOTHRÁKI (SAMOTHRACE) ★★

The **Sanctuary of the Great Gods** on Samothráki once made it the bustling religious centre of the region. Most of today's tourist facilities are found around **Kamariótissa**, a functional rather than 'pretty' port. The picturesque capital, **Chóra**, is set in tiers below a ruined Byzantine castle built on the slopes of **Mt Fengari** (1676m; 5499ft), which is snowcapped except in high summer. The mountain sides are dotted with small villages: one, **Alónia**, has remains of a Roman bath; **Thermá** (Loutrá) is a spa on the opposite side of the mountain and, like Chóra, a starting point for the ascent of what legend claims was Poseidon's vantage point in the Peloponnese War.

The best beach is at **Pachía Ammos** – either reached on foot from **Lákoma** or by caique from the port of **Kamariótissa**. Boat trips circle the island allowing access to the wild southern coast.

THÁSOS ★★

Thásos, an extensively wooded, 398km^2 (154 sq miles) island, is ringed with beaches. It has a moist climate and largely escapes the *meltémi in* summer.

Liménas (Thásos), both capital and a port, is a lively town; many of its various ruins are of marble quarried from Mt Ipsárion (1070m; 3511ft), the highest peak. The Roman Agorá is in the centre of town and the ruins of the Odeon and Sanctuary of Hercules lie near the Agorá.

The Hellenistic theatre above the town on the slopes of the acropolis is used for plays every Saturday in summer. The acropolis has three levels: on the first is a Genoese fortress, on the second there used to be a Temple to Athena Paliouchos – now ruins – and the third level was reputedly a Sanctuary of Pan. Here you can still see the steep 'secret stairway' (presumably used only by the high priests) and the gates which led to the sanctuary.

Beach lovers are spoilt for choice, especially on the east and southern coasts – the road which completely rings the island allows easy access to **Paradise Beach**, **Astrís**, **Potós**, **Pefkári** and **Psilí Ammos**. **Limenária**, the second largest town, is very popular in summer because of its long stretch of well-shaded beach. In high season there are boat trips to **Mt Athos**, a peninsula on the Greek mainland. The monks do not allow any female creatures (humans included) to set foot there. Many houses at **Kástro**, on a high precipice, have been renovated as holiday homes.

Above: *Looming mountains form a dramatic backdrop to the numerous sandy beaches of Thásos.*

FOÚRNI **

Once the home of Byzantine pirates, this rocky, 37km² (14 sq miles) archipelago is that holy grail of island-hoppers – the completely unpoiled island. Foúrni village (**Kámpos**) is delightful, with most people living around the harbour: sandy coves and crystal clear water are within easy walking distance at **Psilí Ammo**, **Elidáki** and **Kámbi**.

Thímena, its tiny neighbour islet, is accessible by caique and has few inhabitants – the only accommodation is under the stars.

PSARÁ *

In 1824, as an example to others contemplating rebellion, the Turks attacked the island, but, rather than surrender, 30,000 people blew themselves up in a hilltop powder magazine to which they had retreated. 3000 people escaped to Evia and founded Néa Psará – a new Psará (better known as Erétria) – they built the new town right on top of the old city of Erétria).

Tourism has not yet caught on in this barren 45km² (17 sq miles) island even though there are fine beaches.

BLACK WINE

Thássos was reputed to be the birthplace of the goddess of agriculture, Demeter. She favoured the island and caused its grapes to produce the famous 'black wine'. Wily Odysseus used a supply of this wine to overcome the one-eyed Cyclops – the giant who had captured the hero and his crew.

The Aegean Islands at a Glance

Spring arrives later in the Aegean isles than anywhere else and **April** and **May** are the best times for naturalists. **May**, **June** and **October** are ideal for walking in the mountains of **Sámos**, **Chíos** and **Lésbos**. Most visitors arrive in late June and the last leave in September. Winters can become surprisingly cool.

Scheduled Olympic flights daily from Athens provide links with Chíos (3 daily), Lésbos (3 in low season to 7 high season), Límnos (2 daily), Sámos (5 daily) and Thásos (daily). **Charter flights** pile into Lésbos and Sámos in summer from northern European destinations and are building up in Chíos and Thásos. **Internal flights** run several times weekly between the islands and also to Thessaloníki. Details are available from the EOT or from Olympic and island airports: **Chíos** Olympic, tel: (0271) 24-515, airport tel: (0271) 23-998; **Lésbos** Olympic, tel: (0251) 28-660, airport tel: (0251) 61-590; **Límnos** Olympic tel: (0254) 22-078, airport tel: (0254) 31-204); **Sámos** airport tel: (0273) 61-219. For **island hopping** there is a weekly service run by *NEL lines* from Thessaloníki (or Kavála) to Rhodes via Límnos, Lésbos, Chíos, Sámos, Ikaría, Pátmos, Kálimnos and Kos.

Agios Efstrátios is linked by **ferries** to Limnos and Rafina (4 weekly). Kavála, Lésbos and Chíos less frequently.
Chíos daily connections with Piraeus, Lésbos and Inoússes, up to 3 weekly to Límnos, Psará and Sámos and with the mainland (Thessaloníki, Kavála and Rafína). Excursion boats run in summer to both Inoússes and Psará. **Port Authority**, tel: (0271) 44-433.
Ikaría has daily ferry links with Piraeus and Sámos. From Agios Kyrikos there is a daily connection with Foúrni and less frequent excursion boats run in summer to Dodecanese islands: Kálimnos, Léros, Lipsí, Mýkonos, Náxos, Pátmos, Páros and Sýros. **Port Authority**, tel: (0275) 22-207.
Lésbos ferries run daily to Chíos and to Piraeus and several times weekly to Agios Efstrátios, Kavála, Límnos, Rafína and Thessaloníki. Weekly ferries run to Ikaría, Pátmos and Sámos. In summer **hydrofoils** provide useful island links with Límnos, Chíos and Sámos (both Vathí and Pithagório), Pátmos and Ikaría and with the mainland (Kavála and Alexandroúpolis). **Port Authority**, tel: (0251) 47-888.
Límnos has ferry connections with Thessaloníki (2 weekly), Piraeus (3 weekly), Chíos, Kavála, Lésbos (4–5 weekly), Agios Efstrátios and Rafína (4 weekly). **Port Authority**, tel: (0254) 22-225.
Sámos ferries tend to call at

both Vathí and Karlóvassi. Daily services run to Piraeus and Ikaría and up to 4 weekly travel to Chíos, Lésbos, Páros and Náxos. Weekly links in season with Sýros and Mýkonos; caiques from Karlóvassi also sail several times weekly to Foúrni. Ferries from the south coast leave from Pithagório with several ferry crossings weekly to Agathonísi, Lipsí, Pátmos, Léros and Kálimnos (allowing connections with the Dodecanese lines) and also several times weekly from Vathí to Ikaría, Páros and Piraeus. In summer, excursion boats to Pátmos and to Turkey (Kusadasi) exploit the large tourist numbers and levy high fares. Anyone arriving in Sámos on a charter flight invalidates the ticket by staying overnight in Turkey. Hydrofoils run in summer from Pythagório to Kos and Pátmos. **Port Authority**, (Sámos) Vathí, tel: (0273) 27-318, Pythagório, tel: (0273) 61-225, Karlóvassi, tel: (0273) 32-343.
Samothráki daily ferries from Alexandroúpolis and weekly links with Limnos and Kavála. Ferries run almost hourly from Kavála to Skála Prínos on Thásos, some continuing to Liménas (Thásos town). About 4 ferries leave daily from Péramos and about 12 daily from Keramotí (near mainland) close to Kavála and dock at Liménas. **Port Authority**, tel: (0551) 41-305.

The Aegean Islands at a Glance

GETTING AROUND

On **Chíos, Lésbos** and **Sámos** the main towns are linked with larger villages by a bus a day – leaving early and returning at the end of the day. On **Ikaría** regular buses connect the two ports but here and on **Límnos** buses only connect villages on the main road once a day so most people share taxis. On **Thásos** there is a bus service linking resorts and beaches. In season boats provide the easiest links between main towns, resorts and the popular beaches. (see page 124 for on-line timetable and bookings).

WHERE TO STAY

Advance booking is advisable especially during peak season when accommodation may be impossible to find on some islands. Most of the islands have three or four main towns with a range of accommodation but some smaller islands have few places to stay. Island villages may offer accommodation, but some don't and others only operate during peak season in summer. The most practical and sensible way of ensuring you secure a room, if you would rather not risk just arriving, is to contact the EOT (Tourist information office) in Athens or the Tourist Police of the island you have chosen to visit (see Useful Contacts in At a Glances). They have lists of hotels, pensions, or rooms available, addresses, telephone numbers, range and prices.

WHERE TO EAT

Wandering around the white-washed alleyways filled with geraniums and bouganvillaea you will often come across a restaurant or taverna which seems hidden. Pop in, and peruse the menu. The Greeks are friendly and do not mind. Restaurants and tavernas in villages or far from the obvious tourist traffic will usually be most rewarding. Continue exploring at the waterfront, which is lined with kiosks, souvlaki stands, bakeries and eating places. Once you have found a venue which appeals, make a reservation or just sit down and order a meal. Watch where the locals eat, as this usually indicates that the food will be excellent, authentic Greek and reasonably priced.

TOURS AND EXCURSIONS

There are many coach trips to inland destinations and archae-ological sites on Chíos, Lésbos and Sámos. Most visitors opt for a day trip to another island or to the Greek and Turkish mainlands from islands near the shore. There are day trips to Philippi for the Royal Tombs of Philip of Macedon, father of Alexander the Great. Turkey is popular – you have to give in your passport in advance and, if on a charter must not stay overnight (this invalidates the ticket). Trips from Sámos allow visits to Kusadasi town and nearby Ephesus and from Chíos you can reach Çesme.

USEFUL CONTACTS

Chíos Tourist Information, tel: (0271) 24-217, **Tourist Police**, tel: (0271) 44-427. **Ikaría Tourist Police**, tel: (0275) 22-222. **Lésbos Tourist Information**, tel: (0251) 42-511; spa at **Loutra Geras**, tel: (0251) 41-503; to view the fossils at **Vrissa**, tel: (0252) 41-201. **E.O.T**, Director of Tourism for Northern Aegean, tel: (0251) 42-511. **Tourist Police**, tel: 22-776. **Límnos Tourist Information**, tel: (0254) 22-996, **Tourist Police**, tel: 22-200. **Sámos Tourist Information** (**Vathí**), tel: (0273) 28-582, **Archaeological Museum**, Samos, tel: (0251) 40-223. **Vathí Tourist Police**, tel: (0273) 27-404, **Pithagório Tourist Police**, tel: (0273) 27-980. **Thásos Tourist Police**, tel: (0593) 22-122.

AEGEAN ISLANDS	J	F	M	A	M	J	J	A	S	O	N	D
AVERAGE TEMP. °F	43	45	50	57	66	73	79	77	70	61	52	46
AVERAGE TEMP. °C	6	7	10	14	19	23	26	25	21	16	11	8
HOURS OF SUN DAILY	4	5	6	7	10	11	12	11	9	7	5	4
RAINFALL ins.	3	2.5	2	2	2	1	1	0.5	1	3	4	4
RAINFALL mm	71	63	47	48	40	26	19	15	28	73	95	93
DAYS OF RAINFALL	5	5	5	6	5	4	2	2	2	5	8	7

9
Evia and The Sporades

Second after Crete, craggy Evia (**Euboea**) is the largest of the islands. Its runs parallel to the mainland for its considerable (175km; 109 miles) length and it is reached from the mainland via a bridge to its capital (**Chalkída**), and numerous shuttle ferries. Because Greeks comprise the bulk of the visitors, prices are realistic and you will find excellent tavernas, restaurants and even authentic oúzerie. There are vivid displays of spring flowers and both **Mt Ochi** (1398m; 4587ft) and **Mt Dírfis** (1745m; 5725ft, snow-capped in winter) and their extensive pine woods offer excellent walking.

The northern **Sporades** scattered head to tail just northeast of Evia, which is a sunken, sickle-shaped extension of the long peninsula running from the south of **Mt Pelion**. There are four main islands: **Skiáthos**, **Skópelos**, **Alónissos** and **Skýros**; plus a number of small, sparsely inhabited islets – **Peristéra**, **Pelágos**, **Yioúra** and **Pipéri** (a reserve for monk seals). **Skiáthos** boasts some of the Aegean's best beaches – golden sands backed by pine forests – and is crowded in summer, as is **Skópelos**. **Alónissos** with its wild scenery is the quietest. Hopping between Skiáthos, Skópelos and Alónissos is easy via regular ferries (or flying dolphin) from **Vólos** on the mainland. **Skýros**, an island with an independent spirit is detached from the others and best reached from **Kími** on Evia. The Sporades have been on trade routes and inhabited since ancient times, yet have few noteworthy archaeological sites.

DON'T MISS

*** Alónissos: the islets and the chance of seeing monk seals which breed in Pipéri.
*** Skiáthos: wonderful beaches, overwhelmingly popular in summer.
** Skópelos: its island walks always in sight of the sea.
** Skýros: the Faltaits Museum with its intriguing collections of folk items: embroidery, porcelain and carved wood.
* Evia: the pleasant walk up Mt Ochi for stunning views and flowers.

Opposite: *An unspoiled island, the beauty of Skópelos is exemplified by Stafílos Beach.*

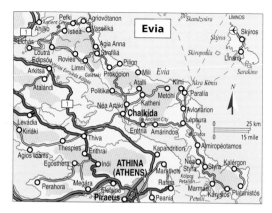

EVIA (EUBOEA) **

Legend has it that Evia became the favourite island of the mythological sea god Poseidon after he sliced it from the mainland with a single blow of his trident. Most tourism is concentrated in a few resorts: **Edipsóu**, **Erétria** **Kárystos** and **Loutrá**. Camping seems to be especially popular with Greek visitors.

Apparently ancient Evia was divided into city states, two of which, **Chalkída** and **Erétria**, grew very powerful through trading in the 8th–7th centuries BC until Mithridiates of Poutus sacked **Erétria** in 87BC.

Chalkída is an unattractive, industrialized town but its museums make a stopover worth considering. The **Archaeology Museum** has items recovered from Erétria including a relief of **Diónysos**, a statue of **Athena** missing the head and a pediment from a **Temple of Apollo**. Open Tues–Sun 08:00–14:30. The **Byzantine Museum** is housed in a delightful 16th-century **Mosque** at the entrance to the **Kástro**, the old Turkish quarter. Within the Kastro is **Agios Paraskevi**, originally a Byzantine basilica but converted to a Gothic Cathedral by the Crusaders in the 14th century. The **Evripós Channel** separating Chalkís from the mainland has long been a tourist curiosity because the tide is unpredictable and can change up to 14 times a day.

The ancient city of **Erétria** lay southeast of Chalkís but in 1824 **Néa Psára** was built on top of it to house the survivors from **Psára** (*see* p.111) after the Turkish massacre. Remains of the ancient city include a **Temple to Apollo Daphnephorus**, a **theatre** and an **acropolis**.

The north is graced with high pine-clad mountains which plunge to pretty coastal villages and delightful beaches. **Loutrá Edipsóu** is one of the most popular **spas** in Greece, with 80 hot springs (71˚C; 160˚F).

CLIMATE

In the **Sporades** summer temperatures are softened by cooling breezes and the skies are clear. Winters are mild but enough rain falls to support extensive pine forests and rather lush vegetation.

Evia, closer to the mainland, has higher, extensively forested mountains and the north, in particular, is very green. Mt Dírfis is snow-capped through winter into early summer.

Edipsos has a lovely wooded bay and there are other beaches nearby between **Ilía** and **Robiés**. Inland the scenery is dramatic and at **Prokópi** suspension bridges carry the trail across the wooded ravines of the **Kleisoúra** valley. **Pílio**, set in rocky country, lies to the east of Prokópi – rooms for rent and several tavernas make it a good base for exploring the region.

In the south there are direct ferry links between **Kárystos** and **Rafína** on the mainland. Kárystos was once famous for its green (*cipollino*) marble and for asbestos. Its waterfront is dominated by a 14th-century fort (**Boúrdzi**) and the backstreets are a fascinating warren. In August the town hosts a lively **wine festival**. The fortifications above the town are known as the **Castel Rosso** (red castle) or **Kókkino Kástro** and are the remains of a fortress built in Byzantine times (1030) and later modified by Franks and Venetians – from the castle you can spot the remains of an aqueduct (*kamáres*).The ancient marble quarries are found near **Myli**, a village set in a ravine – the village is a useful starting point for the ascent of **Mt Ochi** (1398m; 4578ft). About a four hour walk from Myli there is a refuge and beyond it on the path to the summit is a marvellous array of mountain flowers from May through into late August.

The road northwards from **Kárystos** follows the west coast of the island where eagles and other large raptors are a common sight. There is a good sandy beach at **Néa Styra** and ferry connections with **Agia Marína** on the mainland. **Styra**, the old city on the slopes of nearby **Mt Kilósi**, is worth visiting for **Larména**, a massive **Venetian fortress** which dominates it.

> **MT DIRFIS**
>
> The lower slopes of Mt Dírfis (1745m; 5725ft), the highest peak in Evia, are clothed with cool woods of chestnut and pine. A road crosses the shoulder of the mountain to **Stropónes** providing the easiest access to the summit ridge. Above, crocus, white peonies and scarlet lilies are three of the botanical treasures on view.
>
> From **Steni**, with its waterfalls and wooden mountain houses, there is a marked path and challenging walk to the summit.

Below: *Evia's cafés and restaurants have remained haunts for local people.*

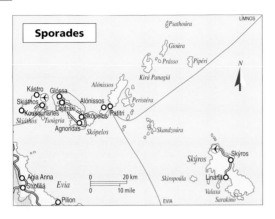

Sporades

Psathoúra

LÍMNOS

Gioúra

Prásso *Pipéri*

N

Kirá Panagiá

Alónissos

Kástro Glóssa

Skiáthos Alónissos *Peristéra*

Koukounáries Loutráki

Skiáthos *Tsoúgria* Skópelos Patitíri

Agnóndas *Skópelos*

Skandzoúra

Skýros Skýros

Agia Anna Skiropoúla Linariá

Stofiliá *Evia* Valaxa

0   20 km

0   10 mile

Pilion EVIA *Sarakino*

SPORADES
ALÓNISSOS **

The first national marine park in Greece was established around **Alónissos** (62km²; 24 sq miles) and the nine islets in its archipelago, to offer protection to the monk seal. A severe earthquake decimated the main town in 1965, citrus production fell and recovery has been very slow. Alónissos town (**Chóra**) has a magnificent setting, Byzantine walls and memorable sunsets. The island's best beaches are reached by caique: **Chrysí Miliá** has a sandy pine-backed beach, **Kokkinó Kástro** is shingle and the site of the former capital of ancient **Ikos** (an early name for the island). Unspoiled beaches are found at **Yérakas**, **Kopelousáko** and **Megaliámos**. For fishing and watersports try **Stení Valá** and **Kalamákia**; snorkellers can find traces of an ancient settlement in the sea near **Agios Dimítrios** and a sunken Byzantine boat at **Agios Petrós**.

THE ARCHIPELAGO

The other islets in the archipelago can be visited by caique from Patitíri but generally only in the high summer season:
• **Peristéra:** lovely, sandy beaches and olive groves.
• **Pelagós (Kyrá Panayía):** abandoned monasteries and thick pine woods.
• **Psathoúra:** home of the Sirens, the mythical songstresses who enchanted Odysseus. The island has a tall lighthouse and the remains of an ancient city beneath the sea.
• **Skantzoúra:** sea caves, coves and excellent fishing.
• **Yioúra:** an ancient breed of goats and the Cyclops cave (from mythology).

Right: *Picturesque Patitíri where the Hellenic Society for the Protection of the Monk Seal has an office at the quay.*

SKIÁTHOS ★★★

Idyllic pine-fringed beaches attract up-market package operators to the island – out of season the wooded 61km² (24 sq miles) island is extraordinarily beautiful and friendly. There is only one main settlement – **Skiáthos town** with its red roofs and sparkling, white buildings. It sits in a bay strewn with islets and its twin harbours have numerous waterfront restaurants including one in the **Venetian Kástro** on the

Boúrtzi promontory. Jam-packed buses ply their trade on the south coast road – with stops for **Megalí Ammos**, **Achládies**, **Kalamáki** and **Kanapítsa**. North coast beaches tend to be less crowded since they are affected by the *meltémi*: **Lalária**, reached by sea, has a natural arch at one end and several sea caves. Paths leading across the island offer an escape from the beach to **Mt Karafiltzanáka** (411m; 1349ft), the highest point of the island and to peaceful **Evangelístria Monastery**. Open daily 8:00–12:00 and 17:00–19:00.

SKÓPELOS ★★★

Tourism has not grown as fast on **Skópelos** as on some of its neighbours. It is a lovely, relaxed 'family' island (96km²; 37 sq miles), with extensive pine forests and pebble beaches. Skópelos town (**Chóra**), the main settlement, is on the exposed northern coast and hydrofoils and ferries make for a small quay at Agnóndas on the southern side in rough weather. The town suffered some damage in the 1965 earthquake but has retained its character. Within the town there are the remains of a **Venetian Kástro** and numerous churches – **Zoödóchos Pigí** has an icon attributed to St Luke.

The town is known for its prunes – plums are dried in a large oven at **Foúrnou Damáskinon**: traditionally crystallized prunes are served with raki.

Above: *Many of the beaches on Skiáthos are pine-fringed. Shown here is Koukounaries and its port.*

ISLAND TRADITIONS

A traditional example of a Skyriot house can be found in the **Archaeology Museum**. The house is an incredible feat of compact living to rival a Romany caravan with space of around 35m² (377sq ft), decorated with beautifully carved furniture, ornate lattice work and inumerable ornamental plates. Since the 16th century plate collecting has been the national Skyriot passion. Open Tuesday–Sunday 08:00–14:30).

The **Faltaits Museum of Folklore** is located in the northeast of Skýros, high on a ridge. It has a marvellous collection of bits and pieces amassed by Manos Faltaits, painter, poet and writer. Its shop has excellent reproductions for sale. Open daily 10:00–13:00; 17:30–20:00.

Above: *Red-roofed
Skópelos town forms
the main settlement and
harbour for the island.*
Below: *Linariá, once a
fishing village, is now
the port of Skýros.*

Regular buses connect Skópelos with coastal settlements – **Stáfilos** has a Minoan tomb, **Pánormos** is a favourite with windsurfers; **Miliá** and **Klimna** tend to be quieter. Other beaches can be reached in high summer by caique – **Glisteri** from Skópelos and **Limonári** from Agnóndas. **Glóssa**, famed for its almonds, is a pretty village above the small port of **Loutráki**.

SKÝROS **

Most of the inhabitants live in the central portion of the island, particularly around the port of **Linariá** and the capital, **Skýros**. To the north the land is well forested but to the south it is dry and barren with steep cliffs. Skýros (**Chóra**) is Cycladic in appearance and its houses

encircle an acropolis surmounted by a kástro. Poet Rupert Brooke is buried at **Tris Boukés** on the southern tip of the island and Brooke Square in Skýros town is named in honour of him.

Sandy **Magaziá** and **Mólos** beaches near the town are the busiest: **Papá ta Chómata** and **Órmos Achílli** are within walking distance. The best beaches are in the north at **Agios Pétros**, **Péfkos**, **Achérouses** and **Agios Fokás**. **Skyropoúla** with its two beaches and cave is reached by caique from **Linariá**.

Evia and the Sporades at a Glance

Evia is delightful in springtime (**March–May**) and **May**, **June** and **October** are ideal for treks in the mountains – Mt Dirfís is snow-capped in **winter** and early **spring**. In **summer**, Evia is popular with Greeks and the Sporades over-run with sun-seekers.

Evia
Ferries from Rafína to the south port of Káristos 3 daily, Rafína to the south port of Marmári 3–4 daily, Agia Marina to the south port of Néa Stíra 5 daily, Skála Oropós to Erétria every half hour, Arkítsa to Loutrá Edipsós 12 daily, Glífa to Agiókambos every two hours. Summer hydrofoils link Loutrá Edipsós and the other Sporades.
Port Authorities:
Erétria, tel: (0221) 62-201.
Káristos, tel: (0224) 22-227.
Marmári, tel: (0224) 31-222.
Edipsós, tel: (0226) 22-464.
Buses every half hour from Liossíon terminal in Athens to Chálkis, Kími, Erétria, Alivéri, Amárinthos and Edipsós. Buses from Mavromatéon terminal in Athens to Rafína to catch ferries to Káristos and Marmári. Trains 19 daily from Larissis Station in Athens to Chálkis.

Sporades
Scheduled Olympic **flights** to the island of Skiáthos from Athens 2 daily, Thessaloníki 3 weekly. Olympic flights to

Skýros from Athens (6 weekly in summer, 2 weekly for the rest of year). Reservations: Athens, tel: (01) 966-6666; Skiáthos, tel: (0427) 22-200; Skýros, tel: (0222) 91-123. There are numerous summer charter flights to Skiáthos.
Ferries from **Skiáthos** to Ay. Konstanínos and Vólos (Thessaly – mainland) daily, to Thessaloníki 1 weekly, to Skýros and Kími (Evia) 1 weekly and to Tínos, Mýkonos, Páros, Thira and Crete 2 weekly. **Port Authority**, tel: ((0427) 22-017.
Alónissos to Ay. Konstanínos, Vólos, Skópelos and Skiáthos daily, to Thessaloníki 3 weekly, to Kími (Evia) 1 per week. **Port Authority**, tel: (0424) 65-595.
Skópelos to Ay. Konstanínos, Vólos, Skiáthos and Alónissos daily, to Thessaloníki 3 weekly, to Kími (Evia) 1 per week. **Port Authority**, tel: (0424) 22-180. Skýros to Kími (Evia) 2 weekly, to Tínos, Mýkonos, Páros, Thíra and Crete 1 per week. **Port Authority**, tel: (0222) 91-475.Hydrofoils operate on these routes in April–October and provide inter-island links with journey times half that of ferries but pricier. Also several times weekly to and from

Thessaloníki, Moudhania (Halkidiki), Pefki (Evia) and Trikeri (Pilion).Ferries to **Skýros** (the boat *FB Lykomides* is well known) from Kimi twice daily June–Sept and once daily the rest of the year.

Buses generally connect with all main villages and mainland towns. Obtain timetables from tourist police on each island. (see page 124 for on-line timetable and bookings).

Evia is very well served with hotels in all its resorts and ports. It is not difficult to find rooms on spec outside the main Greek holiday season in August except in Erétria and Malakónda, which cater for pre-booked package tours.

Tourist Police:
Evia
Chalkis, tel: (0221) 24-662.
Sporades
Alónissos, tel: (0424) 65-205.
Skiáthos, tel: (0427) 21-111.
Skópelos, tel: (0424) 22-235.
Skýros Tourist Police, tel: (0222) 91-274.

SPORADES	J	F	M	A	M	J	J	A	S	O	N	D
AVERAGE TEMP. °F	48	48	52	61	70	79	82	81	75	68	57	50
AVERAGE TEMP. °C	9	9	11	16	21	26	28	27	24	20	14	10
HOURS OF SUN DAILY	4	5	6	7	10	11	12	11	9	7	5	4
RAINFALL ins.	2	2	2	1.5	1	0.5	0	0.5	0	1.5	2.5	2
RAINFALL mm	43	45	54	32	21	10	2	9	3	39	62	58
DAYS OF RAINFALL	9	9	8	7	6	3	1	2	2	6	9	9

Travel Tips

Tourist Information

The National Tourist Organization of Greece (EOT or NTOG) produces a range of free brochures and accommodation directories dealing with each of the major islands (Crete, Rhodes, Corfu) and island groups. **London**, 4 Conduit Street, WIR ODJ, tel: (0171) 734-5997, fax: (0171) 287-1369. **New York**, Olympic Tower, 645 Fifth Avenue, fifth floor, NY 10022, tel: (212) 421-577, fax: (212) 826-6940. **Chicago**, 168 N. Michigan Avenue, Illinois. 60601, tel: (312) 782-1084, fax: (312) 782-1091. **California**, 611 West Street, Suite 2198, Los Angeles. 90017, tel: (213) 626-6696, fax: (213) 489-9744. **Athens**, 2 Amerikís Street, Athens. 10564, tel: (01) 322-3111, fax: (01) 322-4148.

Entry Requirements

From 1995 EU citizens can stay indefinitely; most other visitors (including Australia, Canada, New Zealand and the USA) are allowed up to three months (South Africa: two months), no visas required. Children must either hold their own passports or be entered in parental passports. Visa **extensions** or **work permits** can be obtained from the Aliens Bureau, 9 Halkokondili Street, Athens, tel: (01) 362-8301. Apply well in advance as the bureaucracy is time-consuming. **Temporary jobs** including bar and restaurant work are not difficult to find on the islands – ask in the local *kafeneion*. Graduates hoping to find jobs teaching English will need a TEFL qualification.

Customs

All visitors arriving from **EU countries** can import duty-free no more than 400g of tobacco (300 cigarettes or 75 cigars), 5 litres of wine or 1.5 litres of spirits, 75 grams of perfume or other articles of value up to a total of 55,500 drachmas. Visitors from non EU countries are allowed 250 grams of tobacco (200 cigarettes), 2 litres of wine or 1 litre of alcoholic beverage, 50 grams of perfumes and gifts to a value of 7000 drachmas. In theory, only one camera is allowed per person and articles such as lap-top computers and windsurfers call for some form of assurance from a Greek national resident in Greece that they will be re-exported: in practice there are few problems and foreign nationals are not often stopped.

Health Requirements

No certificates of vaccination are required for visitors.

Getting There

By Air: Direct scheduled flights operate daily to Athens from London and New York (less frequently from Montreal and Toronto) and, in season, to the larger islands which have international airports (Crete, Corfu, Kos, Lésbos, Mýkonos, Skiáthos, Rhodes, Zákinthos). Operators to Athens include Olympic Airways, BA, Virgin Atlantic and TWA.

All **Olympic Airways** flights including **Greek internal flights** arrive at and depart from **Ellinikon Airport West** terminal known to taxi drivers as **Olympiki. East** terminal serves all other **international** and **charter** flights. **Restrictions** on charter flights mean validity for a minimum of three days and maximum of six weeks – you must have an **accommodation voucher** stating name and address of destination (even if mythical). Charter passengers can only visit a neighbouring country (ie Turkey) for a day and not overnight, otherwise the ticket will be invalidated. But, Turkish officials may stamp a piece of paper to avoid putting a Turkish stamp in your passport – this applies to a current visit only: there is no problem with previous trips to Turkey.

By Road: Continuing strife in former Yugoslavia has made the lengthy route by road even less attractive and **buses** from London to Athens go via Italy and the ferry to Greece, taking three days. Contact **Olympic Bus Ltd**, 70 Brunswick Centre, London. WC1 1AE, tel: (0171) 837-9141.

By Rail: There are no longer direct trains from London to Athens but you can go through Italy via Paris and Bologna to Brindisi and take the ferry to Patras. **British Rail International**, tel: (0171) 834–2345.

By Boat: There are regular boats from Brindisi to Corfu, Igouménitsa, Patras and less frequently from other Italian ports: Ancona, Bari and Otranto. To reach Athens either take a ferry from Corfu and then a bus, or a ferry to Patras with connections by bus and train to Athens. Other ferries run to Piraeus from Alexandria, Haifa, Limassol, Syria, Istanbul and less frequently from Odessa.

USEFUL PHRASES	
ENGLISH	*GREEK*
yes	*né*
no	*ochi*
hello	*khérete*
how are you?	*ti kánete?*
goodbye	*adío*
please	*parakaló*
thank you	*efkharistó*
sorry/excuse me	*signómi*
how much is?	*póso iné?*
when?	*poté?*
where?	*pou?*
I'd like	*thélo*
open	*aniktó*
closed	*kleistó*
one	*éna*
two	*dhío*
three	*tría*
four	*téssera*
five	*pénte*
six	*éxi*
seven	*eftá*
eight	*okhtó*
nine	*enniá*
ten	*dhéka*

From Piraeus and several other ports, a bewildering number of **ferries** and **hydrofoils** connect with all the inhabited islands. **Timetables** change annually and the best source of information is the ***Athens Gazette*** (on sale in all bookshops and kiosks in Athens). Details pertaining to each island in a group are given in the relevant **At a Glance**. In general, hydrofoils are twice as fast as conventional ferries but double the price.

What to Pack

In summer, light-weight cotton T-shirts and shorts suffice most of the time. Out of season evenings can get surprisingly cool on the islands so pack a pullover (even waterproofs) . In more up-market resorts you may want smarter clothes for evening but leave the tuxedo at home. Hats, sun glasses and a UV protection sun cream are advisable during the day.

Money Matters

Currency: national currency is the drachma with notes in denominations of 50, 100, 500, 1000 and 5000 and coins of 1, 2, 5, 10, 20, 50 and 100.

Currency exchange: other than on the remotest islands (where you take drachmas with you) you can change money in a bank (*trápeza*), post office or shipping agent. Post Offices change cash, travellers cheques and Eurocheques and charge less commission than banks. In major resorts the numbers of ACT's (automatic cash tellers) grow yearly.

Travellers cheques: especially Thomas Cook and American Express are accepted in all banks and post offices (passport needed as ID). Cash transfers are best handled by major banks in Athens or Piraeus.

Credit Cards: allow cash withdrawals at banks and ACT's. **Visa** is handled by the Commercial Bank of Greece and **Access/Mastercard** by the National Bank of Greece.

Tipping: a 10–15% service charge is added to restaurant bills, but Greeks usually leave change as a tip. Taxi drivers, porters and cleaners welcome a tip, usually 125 drachma depending on the service offered.

VAT (FPA – Fóros Prostitheménis Axias): is 6%, 13% or 18% depending on which services or products are provided.

Accommodation

From June to early September most island hotels are geared to the pre-booked package trade – look for last minute bargains from your local travel agents. Prices are government controlled according to category (Luxury, A, B, C, D and E). By law, these rates have to be displayed in each hotel room. On smaller islands many hotels close out of season but people are glad to rent rooms and are open to gentle bargaining.

The **Tourist Police** and **NTOG office** have lists of available accommodation (including pensions) on any island and locals stand on the harbour to meet ferries and offer rooms for rent. Greek ladies are house proud and the accommodation will be simple but spotless.

Youth Hostels: both official (curfew) and informal (no curfew) exist on many islands – an International Membership Card is available from the Greek Association of Youth Hostels, 4 Dragatsabfou Street, Athens, tel: (01) 323-4107.

Camping: is offically permitted only on authorized sites – on smaller islands be guided by local attitudes over sleeping out on beaches. If police insist you move – be polite and do it. Very little special provision is made for **disabled visitors** and their companions as yet. Visitors with disabilities should contact the NTOG.

Eating Out

Most visitors eat in restaurants (Estiatoria) or tavernas. In the latter diners usually begin with starters (mezédhes) and follow with meat and fish courses. Some tavernas specialize in fish (Psarotaverna) or grills (Psistaria). Greeks eat very late and do not hurry a meal.

Transport

Boat: inter-island services are operated by ferry and hydrofoil (rough seas can play havoc with hydrofoil schedules). To many smaller islands there are caique services, and **taxi boats** operate between ports/resorts and other beaches. Timetables can be consulted and bookings made quickly and easily via the Internet. The centralized service is accessed via http://www.greekferries.gr which allows you to look at local and international services. Domestic lines include Anev,

Minoan, Poseidon, Strintzis and Superfast. Agapitos, which operates in the Cyclades, can be accessed directly via http://agapitos-ferries.com

Air: inter island links available between those islands with airports (see **At a Glance** under each relevant section).

Road: on the larger and more popular islands local **buses** are a reliable mode of transport for visitors and locals – they make stops for major beaches. On smaller islands buses might be one a day between towns – leaving early and returning at the end of the working day.

Taxis: are a widely used on all the islands – agree on a price before the journey or check the meter is running. Sharing is common practice – each person pays full rate for the part of the journey they undertake.

Car hire: charges and fuel costs are high in Greece and worthwhile only on larger islands as part of a 'fly-drive'. Non-EC citizens need an International Driving Licence. Always pay the supplement for collison damage waiver to avoid potential problems later. Assistance can be sought via the Automobile and Touring Club of Greece (ELPA). Athens: 2–4 Messoghion Avenue, tel: (01) 779-1615 or 6 Amerikis and Panepistimiou Street, tel: (01) 368-8632. On Crete: Hánia (0821) 26-059 and Iráklion, tel: (081) 289-440. Maximum speed in built up areas is 50kph (30mph) and in other areas 80kph (50mph). Diesel and Super, Apli and Unleaded petrol are available on all the major islands.

CONVERSION CHART		
FROM	**TO**	**MULTIPLY BY**
Millimetres	Inches	0.0394
Metres	Yards	1.0936
Metres	Feet	3.281
Kilometres	Miles	0.6214
Kilometres square	Square miles	0.386
Hectares	Acres	2.471
Litres	Pints	1.760
Kilograms	Pounds	2.205
Tonnes	Tons	0.984
To convert Celsius to Fahrenheit: x 9 ÷ 5 + 32		

Car hire outlets for Avis, Budget and Hertz operate at major airports and in Athens along Singrou Avenue. If you take your car to Greece 1 year's free use is permitted by customs (with a 4 month extension on request) – Australians and N. American citizens are allowed two years.

Motorcycles, Bicycles and Scooters: are cheap and fun for getting around the smaller islands. Check the machine carefully first (especially brakes) and wear protective clothing – accidents are common.

Hitch hiking: is generally safe

and accepted, if not speedy. **Tours:** numerous travel companies offer specialized tours geared towards antiquities and wildlife. A list of all operators is provided by the **NTOG.**

Business Hours

Opening hours vary according to the nature of the business and are confusing even for Greeks. Generally Monday, Wednesday and Saturday from 09:00–14:30. Tuesday, Thursday and, Friday from 09:00–17:00. In many resorts, supermarkets open at 09:00 and close at 22:00 or later.

Banking hours are: Monday-Thursday 08:00–14:00 and Saturday 08:00–13.00. Arrive early as queues can be long.

Time Difference

Greece is two hours ahead of Greenwich Mean Time, one hour ahead of Central European Time and seven hours ahead of US Standard Winter Time. Clocks go forward one hour on the last weekend in March, and then back on the last Sunday in September.

Communications

Post: there are post offices (*tachidromío*) and money changing facilities in large and small towns and at all ports, providing normal postal services (including *poste restante*). English is often spoken. Post can be slow (up to three weeks for a card) and express, though more expensive, is much faster. Stamps (*grammatósima*) are also sold at kiosks and tourist shops, and

post boxes are bright yellow. **Telephones:** International calls can be made from hotels or more cheaply from offices of the OTE (*Organsimós Telefikoinonía Elládos*) – there is at least one on every island allowing you to dial direct or make collect calls. For the UK dial 0044 and then the area code (omitting the zero at the beginning); for the US dial 001. Cardphones have replaced payphones everywhere – phonecards are sold at *periptera* (1000 drachmas per 100 units). There is more chance of getting through to Athens from islands in the evenings – wait for a series of six clicks after the area code to reduce chances of having to redial endlessly.

Electricity

Mains voltage is 220AC supplied @ 50Hz. Plugs are continental 2-pin – universal adaptors fit them. US appliances need converters.

Weights and Measures

The metric system is used throughout, plus, occasionally, measures from the early Ottoman occupation, such as the *oká* (1.3kg or 2.8lb) divided into 400 *drams* and the *strémma* (0.25 acre).

Health Precautions

Visitors to the islands should make sure that their tetanus protection is up to date. Don't underestimate the strength of the sun – even short exposures to sensitive skins can leave a child or adult very sunburnt and in agony.

GOOD READING

- Alibertis, Antoine (1994) *The Samaria Gorge and its Plants,* Iráklion, Crete.
- Buttler, Karl (1991) *Field Guide to the Orchids of Britain and Europe,* Crowood Press, Swindon.

  Classics (Penguin Classic)
- Homer *The Odyssey* and *The Illiad*
- Herodotus *The Histories*
- Pausanias *The Guide to Greece* (2 vols)
- Plutarch *The Age of Alexander, Plutarch on Sparta, The Rise and Fall of Athens*
- Thucydides *History of the Peloponnese War*
- Xenophon *The History of My Times*
- Durrell, Gerald *My Family and other Animals,* Viking/ Penguin.
- Durrell, Lawrence (1961) *The Greek Islands,* Viking/ Penguin.

- Durrell Lawrence (1960) *Reflections on a Marine Venus,* Faber and Faber.
- Fowles, John (1977) *The Magus,* Cape, London.
- Hardy, David A. (1983) *Greek language and Peoples,* BBC Publications.
- Kazantzakis, Nikos *Zorba the Greek*
- *Christ Recrucified*
- *The Fratricides*
- *Freedom or Death,* Faber and Faber/ Simon and Schuster.
- Levi, Peter (1980) *Atlas of the Greek World,* Phaidon, Oxford.
- Renault, Mary (1986) *The Last of the Wine* Sceptre, London.
- Seferis, George (1924–1955) *Collected Poems,* Anvil Press/ Princetown UP.
- Seferis, George (1984) *Flowers of Greece* Papeco, Athens.

Remember to use sun hats, high protection sun cream and practise sensible sunbathing. The only truly venomous **snake** is the viper (*kufi*) – anti-serum available locally; large black Montpellier snakes are harmless to humans. At the seaside, **weaver fish** can lay hidden beneath sand in shallow water with their poisonous spines protruding. Excessive olive oil can cause stomach upsets – retsina, coca-cola and fresh parsley (*mitanós*) can all help. Although standards of hygiene are generally high in Greece, water shortages (and poor Greek plumbing) on islands don't make things easy in summer. Always carry your own toilet paper.

Tap water is safe to drink but might be brackish on some islands – bottled water is widely available.

Health services

There is a reciprocal agreement giving free medical treatment to EC residents (UK visitors should take form E111 from the DHSS). Make sure your **travel insurance** offers medical cover plus the provision of an 'air taxi'. Many doctors speak good English but equipment in some Greek hospitals is often behind what is commonplace at home.

Personal Safety

Theft is still not commonplace on Greek islands although it has increased in tourist destinations like Ios in recent years. In cities, Greeks blame the marked increase in car theft and stealing from rooms (now no different from other European cities) on an influx of poverty-stricken Albanians. Generally harassment of lone females is low-key for a Mediterranean country outside the resorts and many women explore the islands alone – a sharp *afistime* (leave me alone) or *fiyete* (go away) usually suffices. Greek friends might equip you with a few more forceful phrases. Much has been made in the western press about incidents of rape – they horrify Greeks as much as anyone because crime is so rare here.

Emergencies

Ambulance: tel: 166 anywhere in Greece.
Police: *see* Tourist Police under **Useful Contacts** in every **At a Glance** section.

Etiquette

In monasteries and churches, dress with decorum: no shorts or bare tops for men; women should cover bare arms or legs so as not to cause offence or be offended when admission to a place of worship is refused. Nudism is forbidden by law except in designated areas – topless sunbathing is permitted on most of the beaches.

Language

Greek is the main language of daily conversation, notices in shops and on signposts on the islands. Ferry destinations at ports are in Greek capitals. English is learned at school and many Greeks speak a little German. A few words of Greek on your part is welcomed.

INDEX